People of Purpose

80 PEOPLE WHO HAVE MADE A DIFFERENCE

ARNOLD B. CHEYNEY

EMERITUS PROFESSOR
UNIVERSITY OF MIAMI

Good Year Books

An Imprint of Addison-Wesley Educational Publishers, Inc.

Good Year Books
are available for most basic curriculum subjects
plus many enrichment areas. For more Good Year
Books, contact your local bookseller or educational
dealer. For a complete catalog with information about other
Good Year Books, please write:

Good Year Books
1900 East Lake Avenue
Glenview, IL 60025

Book design by Foster Design.
Text copyright © 1998 Good Year Books,
    an imprint of Addison-Wesley Educational Publishers Inc.
All Rights Reserved.
Printed in the United States of America.

ISBN 0-673-36371-6

1 2 3 4 5 6 7 8 9 - EB - 06 05 04 03 02 01 00 99 98

DEDICATION

TO THE STAFF OF THE WOOSTER PUBLIC LIBRARY

WOOSTER, OHIO

ACKNOWLEDGEMENTS

In my experience, gracious men and women are attracted to libraries. This is particularly true, in my emeritus state, as I daily step into the Wooster, Ohio, public library. Staff members share books by the bagful with me and go out of their way to be accommodating. I imagine similar scenes in heaven.

My gratitude, also, to Bobbie Dempsey and Jenny Bevington at Good Year Books, for persevering with me until the proposal for this manuscript finally became reality. I could not ask to work with two finer professionals. And to Jeanne, my wife, thanks for the hours of editing, suggesting, and encouraging for this and the many other publications we have been privileged to do.

Reading biographies is an experience in walking in others' shoes, feeling their rejections and their triumphs and making them ours. These real people of our recent past and living present proclaim to us how those with purpose make a difference. These people are life-and-breath models children need. There is much in these forty men and forty women to lift our spirits. Let your imagination and that of children touch the lives of the persons found in *People of Purpose*.

Be careful as you read, for these people challenge our complacency. People of purpose view themselves in the light of their potential and not of their circumstances. They expect no less of you. Consider the animosity that greeted their ideas:

Suffrage for all: "Nonsense!"
Abolish slavery: "There have always been slaves!"
Protect the environment: "We have to make a living!"
Mosquitoes carry sickness: "What stupidity!"
One can carry light in a bottle: "Are you serious?"
Unseen microorganisms cause disease: "Ridiculous!"
We were here first, eons before you: "Tough! I'm bigger."

Undaunted by criticism, these people of purpose set out to overcome the challenges they faced.

Pondering the biographical lives of purposeful people gives one understanding of the people portrayed. This studying of others can lead us to consider ourselves in the light of their lives. Perhaps their lives will enable all of us to stretch our minds in our quest for understanding. Let their exemplary behavior clash with our failures so that our own value systems can gain strength.

This does not mean approval of all of their acts, for their humanity sticks out its jagged edges from time to time for all to see. Any darker areas they may have only accent their successes as our measure of hope. Their lives come into personal focus at the point we say to a friend, "Did you know that _____ had this problem, and in spite of it, she did this about it? . . ."

How to Use This Book

People of Purpose is intended as a bridge to further reading; the biographies, therefore, are short by design. After children read and reflect on the ones found here, encourage them to go to the library with its many biographies, reference works, and films. Use the index on page 165 for help in comparing and contrasting the ones here with other people of purpose with similar interests and careers.

Suggest to children that they keep a journal as they read the biographies. Their journals will help them when they react to the questions and activities found at the end of each biography. Or you, as parent or teacher, may read a biography aloud each day and then discuss it. The biographies are reproducible for individuals, small groups, and classrooms. Children can present them orally—as narrative or dramatic presentations—to younger and older children and to adults.

CONTENTS

v

People of Purpose

ABIGAIL SMITH ADAMS ★ 1744–1818

Supporter of Women's Rights and Letter Writer

Abigail always wanted to know about everything. Her mother taught her to read, write, and do arithmetic in addition to teaching her about cooking, housekeeping, and gardening. Abigail's father, a Congregational minister in Weymouth, Massachusetts, encouraged her to read the books in his library.

John Adams, a young lawyer from neighboring Braintree, was impressed with seventeen-year-old Abigail. Originally, he had thought he would remain single—and then he talked to Abigail. She was smart and practical.

When Abigail was about twenty and John twenty-nine, Reverend Smith, her father, performed the marriage ceremony. The couple moved to John's farm in Braintree (now called Quincy), and soon children were on the way.

John was often away from home for long periods of time because of his duties with the Continental Congress, a convention of delegates from the American colonies. The Revolutionary War broke out in 1775. Schools were closed, so Abigail taught her children at home. The oldest children, Abigail (nicknamed Nabby) and John Quincy, learned French and Latin from their mother. The younger boys, Charles and Tommy, were taught to read and write. Meanwhile, Abigail wrote letters constantly to her husband and others.

Abigail wrote to her husband on March 31, 1776, when he was organizing a new government in the Continental Congress. That letter became famous as a plea for women's rights. She wrote: "I long to hear you have declared an independancy—and by the way in the new Code of Laws which I suppose it will be necessary for you to make I desire you would Remember the Ladies, & be more generous & favourable to them than your ancestors. Do not put such unlimited power into the hands of the Husbands. Remember, all Men would be tyrants if they could."

After the war Abigail sailed to England, where John was the new United States ambassador. The new United States government had little money to pay its ambassadors. When they entertained, Abigail served humble American dishes and did her own shopping. The English press made fun of John and Abigail.

In 1797 John Adams became the second president of the United States. The ever-practical Abigail hung her washing to dry in the vacant East Room of the White House because there was no other place provided.

Abigail continued to write letters; more than two thousand of them still exist. Abigail asked her husband to burn them, but fortunately he did not. Through her many letters we now have a better understanding of what life was like in our young republic.

Abigail died of typhoid fever just two weeks before her seventy-fourth birthday. She was the only woman to have been the wife of one president of the United States and the mother of another president. Her son John Quincy Adams became the sixth president in 1825.

1. Make a list of five words that describe Abigail Adams. Compare your list with a classmate's.
2. With a partner, reread the part from Abigail's letter that begins, "I long to hear. . . ." Discuss why Abigail would say, "all Men would be tyrants if they could." Why do you think she wrote that?
3. If you could ask Abigail one question, what would it be?

SOCIAL STUDIES

1. Find a letter written by Abigail Adams. Read it several times and then explain it in your own words for the class.
2. Abigail and John were known as people of integrity. Name some people in today's government who are known as people of integrity.
3. Why are the ideas of the president's wife (or husband) important?
4. Pretend your husband or wife is the president of the United States and you are away on a diplomatic tour around the world. Write a letter to him or her, stating several things you think it is important for him or her to do as president.

FURTHER READING

Bober, Natalie S. *Abigail Adams: Witness to a Revolution*. New York: Atheneum Books for Young Readers, 1995.

Osborne, Angela. *Abigail Adams: Women's Rights Advocate*. American Women of Achievement Series. New York: Chelsea House Publishers, 1989.

Peterson, Helen Stone. *Abigail Adams: "Dear Partner."* New York: Chelsea Juniors, 1991.

Wagoner, Jean Brown. *Abigail Adams: Girl of Colonial Days*. New York: Aladdin Books, 1992.

JANE ADDAMS 1860–1935

Social Reformer, Pacifist, Women's Rights Advocate

Jane Addams tossed and turned in bed. She could not sleep, for she had told a lie during the day. Quietly, she made her way downstairs to her father's room and gently shook him awake. Fearful of what he might do or say, she told him what she had done. He looked at her and told her he was glad he had a little girl who felt so bad about telling a lie that she would come to her father about it. Then he sent her back to bed. As an adult, Jane's honesty and integrity would benefit thousands of needy people.

While traveling, she was moved by the situation of the homeless in London, England. She was impressed by the efforts of some people to help them. She went back to Europe two years later with the purpose of learning more so she might help the homeless in the United States.

After she returned Jane bought a run-down mansion on Chicago's Halsted Street. With the help of Ellen Gates Starr and volunteers, the large house was made ready for those who lived in the Italian neighborhood, where several families often lived together in one room. In May 1889 she named it Hull House and opened it for clubs, classes, and lectures.

At that time there were no laws about children working. Children as young as five years of age worked twelve to sixteen hours a day, six days a week in factories. Small children were hired to work around the dangerous machines because they could squeeze around them. Many children were hurt, and some lost their lives. Jane encouraged politicians to make laws against such abuse.

In her neighborhood the streets were a mess because the garbage was not collected regularly. Jane applied for the job of ward garbage inspector. It was the only job she ever took for pay—one thousand dollars per year. She reported that the collection crews were not doing their job. Even though the local politicians passed a rule that eliminated her position, she had made her point: the garbage was picked up. Shortly thereafter, the death rate in Jane's district dropped from third to seventh because of the improved sanitary conditions.

People all over the world heard about the things Jane was doing to improve the lives of the poor. She wrote books and articles, spoke, and became an ardent worker for peace. Many people learned about her in Germany, France, and Japan because her autobiography, *Twenty Years at Hull House*, was published in their languages.

When Jane Addams was seventy-one, she was only the second woman ever to be honored with the Nobel Peace Prize. She encouraged President Franklin Roosevelt to appoint a woman as secretary of labor— Frances Perkins. Frances was the first woman in the cabinet of a president of the United States. Frances had volunteered at Hull House some years before.

Because of Jane Addams, neighborhood centers or settlement houses are now located across the country. Among the issues they deal with are immigration, child and family welfare, civil rights, and housing.

READING

1. Imagine yourself as a newspaper editor. Write three headlines describing the work of Jane Addams as a social worker.
2. What does it mean to be a "social reformer"? With a partner or group, choose one aspect of your neighborhood or town that needs reform. Brainstorm up to ten ways to improve the problem.
3. What would happen if garbage were not collected for several months in your neighborhood? Draw a picture to describe the scene.
4. If you could encourage the president of the United States to do something, what would it be? Write him a letter.

SOCIAL STUDIES

1. On which of the Great Lakes is Chicago located? Read about Chicago in a reference book and share three interesting facts with your class.
2. Who was the first woman to be honored with the Nobel Peace Prize? What country was she from?
3. Jane Addams was concerned that children had to work long hours around dangerous machines. Write a paragraph of fifty words on what Jane would say if she could come back and see how children in the United States are treated now.
4. With a group, make a list of several agencies in your town that care for people who are poor or in need of help. Visit one of the agencies or have a representative come to your class.

FURTHER READING

Kittredge, Mary. *Jane Addams*. New York: Chelsea House Publishers, 1988.

Schraff, Anne. *Women of Peace: Nobel Peace Prize Winners*. Hillside, NJ: Enslow Publishers, Inc., 1994.

Wheeler, Leslie A. *Jane Addams*. Englewood Cliffs, NJ: Silver Burdett Press, 1990.

KONRAD ADENAUER ★ 1876–1967

Chancellor of the Federal Republic of Germany

Christmas would soon arrive in Germany. Konrad looked forward to the holiday. Then in November his mother gathered him, his sister, and two brothers around her. "Children," she said, "we do not have enough money to buy a Christmas tree this year." The Adenauer children were saddened. "But," she continued, "I'll let you vote. If we go through the month of December without meat on Sundays, we can take the money we save and buy a tree." The children easily agreed to go without meat on Sundays. Konrad never forgot the lesson he learned that day.

His father, who was orphaned as a small child and able to get only an elementary education, was quiet and strict. He wanted his boys to get the education he was not able to receive. To do this, he taught them at home, and they were able to skip a grade in school. He made sure they studied. If a fire engine went by the house, the children could not get up to watch it. They had to study.

Konrad's mother took in boarders to help meet the cost of raising four children. One boarder died and left some money to the Adenauers. It was put in a fund to send the children to college.

Konrad became a law student in 1894. To help himself through school, he joined a Catholic students' association. Since Konrad knew how to budget money, the students gave him theirs to handle. He put them on a strict budget and would not give them a penny more than they were allowed.

In the years that followed, Konrad took a job in Cologne and married Emma Weyers who, like Konrad, was a devout Catholic. Konrad wanted to live in the country and tend a flower garden and invent things. His first invention was a steam engine. Then he heard there was a job open in Cologne as deputy mayor, and he applied for it. He was only thirty years old when he got the job. Eleven years later, in 1917, Konrad, then forty-one, became lord mayor of Cologne and the youngest lord mayor of any city in all of Germany.

In 1933 Hitler came to power and removed Konrad from his position. He moved his family to a small town and kept in touch with only a few friends. The Nazis also put Konrad in prison during World War II a number of times.

Because Konrad was mayor of Cologne from 1917 to 1933, many Germans knew and respected him. Thus, in 1949, at the age of seventy-three, he became chancellor of West Germany. He helped Germany recover economically from a devastating war and Hitler's tyrannical leadership. He united Germany with the Western powers. He recognized that Germany under Hitler was responsible for the crimes against the Jews, and under his leadership, Germany compensated the Jewish state of Israel for these crimes. Konrad was respected by the people of West Germany and around the world. He died in his home in 1967, knowing that he had done all he could for his beloved Germany.

1. What kinds of lessons did Konrad Adenauer learn as a child? How do you think they prepared him to be a great leader?
2. List the names of three of your relatives or friends who you think would enjoy reading a biography of Konrad Adenauer. Why would they enjoy reading about him?
3. Have you ever had to give up something in order to gain something more worthwhile? Write a paragraph about it. Then compare it to the decision the Adenauer family made to go without meat for a few weeks so they could have a Christmas tree.

SOCIAL STUDIES

1. In what section of Germany is Cologne located? Read about Cologne in a reference book and choose two interesting facts about the city to share with the class.
2. What countries and seas surround present-day Germany?
3. After World War II, Germany was divided into two parts. What year did the Berlin Wall, separating East and West Germany, come down? With a small group, read about the wall in a reference book. Draw a picture or build a model of it.

4. Konrad became chancellor at the age of seventy-three. What does that tell you about how the German people felt about his ability to lead? Do you think there should be a mandatory age for retirement?

FURTHER READING

Cudlipp, Edythe. *Konrad Adenauer.* World Leaders Past & Present Series. New York: Chelsea House Publishers, 1985.

Epler, Doris M. *The Berlin Wall: How It Rose and Why It Fell.* Brookfield, CT: The Millbrook Press, 1992.

McKenna, David. *East Germany.* New York: Chelsea House Publishers, 1988.

SUSAN B. ANTHONY ★ 1820–1906

Organizer of the Woman Suffrage Movement

Susan B. Anthony learned a valuable lesson in September of 1840, at the age of twenty, when she applied for a teaching position. The people who ran the school wanted her because they knew she was a good teacher. The man they had let go in the spring was incompetent. He had earned $10 a week, but they hired Susan for $2.50 a week because she was a woman. Susan did not forget that. She went on to be a champion for the rights of women.

Susan's father brought her up in the Quaker belief that women are equal to men. She held that message close to her heart and worked her whole life to persuade others to believe it.

As she grew older, Susan formed the Woman's State Temperance Society of New York. During the Civil War, she supported the abolition of slavery. When the Fifteenth Amendment to the Constitution was written, she became very concerned. Black men were given the privilege of voting but not black women or white women!

Susan and Elizabeth Cady Stanton became a team. Like Susan, Elizabeth believed that it was unfair for women not to have the right to vote. They were half the population; why shouldn't they vote too?

Elizabeth had seven children and could not always travel because of family responsibilities, so she wrote speeches and Susan gave them. Susan traveled all over the United States by stagecoach, giving speeches. During the winter, she often went by horse-drawn sled.

In 1872 she got herself arrested by voting in a national election. The judge fined her one hundred dollars. She said she would never pay the fine, and she never did. Instead, she went around the country speaking on the question, "Is It a Crime for a U.S. Citizen to Vote?"

With Elizabeth, Susan started a newspaper called *The Revolution*. They decided that this was a good way to promote the causes in which women were interested. But it went bankrupt after two years for lack of subscribers and financial help. Susan lectured throughout the country for ten years to pay off the debt of ten thousand dollars. She would not declare bankruptcy to get out of the debt. Even her critics applauded her for this.

Later in her life she wrote a five-volume *History of Woman's Suffrage*. When she was seventy-four, she was traveling up to one hundred miles a week and speaking five or six nights each week. In February of 1906, when she was eighty-six, she made her last public utterance. It ended with these words: ". . . with such women consecrating their lives, failure is impossible!"

At the time of her death, only four states granted women the right to vote. Fourteen years later, on August 18, 1920, the Nineteenth Amendment was ratified and became part of the Constitution. This amendment, also called the Susan B. Anthony Amendment, states: "The right of citizens of the United States to vote shall not be denied or abridged by the United States or by any state on account of sex."

1. Choose a writing companion. Each write a sentence telling what you liked best about Susan B. Anthony. Exchange sentences and write to your partner explaining why you agree or disagree with his or her sentence.
2. Write a letter to the principal of the school where Susan worked for $2.50 a week. How much should Susan have been paid, and why?
3. Quakers have long believed women and men are equal. What special beliefs do you have?

SOCIAL STUDIES

1. How would you answer the question, "Is it a crime for a United States citizen to vote?" Is there anyone in the United States that should not be allowed to vote?
2. Read the amendments to the Constitution in a reference book or textbook. Which one is the most important to you and which is the least important to you?
3. Even though Susan did not live to see the Nineteenth Amendment ratified by the states, do you think she thought of herself as a failure? Would you think yourself a failure if you worked all your life for something that never came to pass?

4. Are there some jobs that only men or only women should do? Which ones? Why?

FURTHER READING

Levin, Pamela. *Susan B. Anthony: Fighter for Women's Rights*. New York: Chelsea Juniors, 1993.

Weisberg, Barbara. *Susan B. Anthony: Woman Suffragist*. New York: Chelsea House Publishers, 1988.

JOHNNY APPLESEED (JOHN CHAPMAN)   1774–1845

Ohio River Valley Pioneer

John Chapman's father, Captain Nathaniel Chapman, fought in the Revolutionary War as a minuteman at the Battle of Bunker Hill. John was just two years old when his mother died while his father was away. In his early twenties John set out for western Pennsylvania and Ohio.

John's religious nature made him want to share his faith. The Christian doctrine of Emmanuel Swedenborg, a Swedish theologian, influenced him. He carried his Bible and books by Swedenborg on his travels. Apples also interested John. He supported himself by developing apple orchards in Ohio and Indiana.

John would set up apple nurseries ahead of the settlers who were moving into the Ohio Valley. The land on which he worked was mostly unclaimed or unoccupied. He took his seeds, planted them, and often built fences of brush around them so deer and other animals could not eat the tender shoots that came up. Later, he came back and took the small trees to settlers and sold them.

Often when he visited settlers, he gave them apple seeds to plant themselves. When they offered to feed him, he would not sit down until he was assured that the children had enough to eat. Then at night he read from his Bible and spoke about his faith. He often went barefoot and used the bag he carried for a pillow. John Chapman became better known as "Johnny Appleseed." In fact, sometimes he even signed his name as Johnny Appleseed.

The settlers needed apples, not only for eating but also for the many other products into which apples could be made. Apples provided vinegar and preservatives for pickles and preserves. The settlers welcomed apple butter and mincemeat for their diets. They also used apples to barter for eggs, chickens, deerskins, and beaver pelts. They buried apples in the ground in late autumn and dug them up again in the early spring, cold and delicious to eat. Settlers also shipped them down the Ohio Valley to markets on the Mississippi River and then on to New Orleans.

John became a friend to Native Americans and settlers alike. When necessary, he warned the settlers that they were in danger from hostile Native Americans, and the settlers would run to the nearest blockhouse for safety.

Soon stories were told far and wide about a man called Johnny who carried appleseeds to the settlers and helped them. Often the stories got exaggerated and became folk tales. Here are a few of the tales that were told about him: John put out his campfire because mosquitoes and moths were burned by the shooting flames. John wore a tin pan for a hat and also used it to cook his food. John took off a shoe and carried it because the shoe had crushed a worm.

There are many other such stories. But the things we know as fact come from government records still on file. When John died, he owned or leased nearly 1,200 acres of land in what is now Ohio and Indiana. He helped many people. He often spoke about his faith and he was genuinely honest. John Chapman, affectionately known as Johnny Appleseed, died near Fort Wayne, Indiana, in March 1845.

People of Purpose

1. Does Johnny Appleseed remind you of any-one you know? Who? In what way?
2. What are some things you would like to know for sure about John Chapman?
3. What do the folktales about Johnny say about the kind of person he was? Make a list of his qualities.
4. Draw a picture of Johnny Appleseed and add a caption that would be a good title for his biography.

SOCIAL STUDIES

1. What are some varieties of apples you enjoy eating? Look in an encyclopedia for pictures of them and others. Make a list of ten kinds of apples and where they come from.
2. On a map, trace the route that people used to send apples by boat to New Orleans from Ohio and Indiana. What rivers would the boat use?
3. Find Fort Wayne, Indiana, on a map. Read about the city in a reference book. Does your reference book tell you how it got its name? Don't tell your classmates. Let them find out for themselves.

4. Create a television commercial to advertise selling apples grown from a tree planted by Johnny Appleseed. Draw scenes from the commercial and show it to the class. Or make a videotape with some classmates and play it for the class.

FURTHER READING

Greene, Carol. *John Chapman: The Man Who Was Johnny Appleseed*. Rookie Biography Series. Chicago, IL: Childrens Press, 1991.

Le Sueur, Meridel. *Little Brother of the Wilderness*. Stevens Point, WI: Holy Cow! Press, 1987.

CORAZON AQUINO ★ 1933–

President of the Philippines

Corazon "Cory" Cojuangco met her husband-to-be, Benigno "Ninoy" Aquino, Jr., for the first time when they were both about nine years old. The event was a birthday party for Ninoy's father. Cory and Ninoy's fathers were friends and congressmen in the Philippines. Cory was the sixth child in a family of eight children.

Deep religious convictions ruled Cory's life. People remembered Cory for many kind acts, including walking a blind girl to class.

On her return to the Philippines from studying in the U.S., she took law courses. But then she met Ninoy again. He was now a journalist. They were married in 1954 when they were twenty-one years old. For the next three decades, Cory remained a loyal wife and mother. The couple had four daughters and a son. Cory spent her time helping her husband begin his political career.

During this time, Ferdinand Marcos became president of the Philippines. Many believed that Marcos would be defeated if he ran for president against Ninoy. Marcos suspended the constitution, imposed martial law, and arrested Ninoy for murder, subversion, and illegal possession of firearms. Cory's husband spent seven and a half years in prison. She called this time "her great suffering." Cory visited Ninoy once or twice each week during the visiting hours.

Ninoy went on a hunger strike in jail for thirty-nine days and became ill. He had a heart attack and Marcos allowed him to go to the United States for a triple-bypass heart opera-tion. He recovered and then taught at Harvard University. Cory remembers those three years as their happiest. Upon his return home to the Philippines, Ninoy was assassi-nated. He had planned to run for president again.

The Philippine economy got worse and worse after Ninoy's death. Inflation increased and the government was not able to make interest payments on its foreign debts.

After much prayer and discussion with friends, Cory decided to run for president against Marcos. She often said there were many other people much more capable than she. But the Filipino people wanted her to be president. They did not care if she just thought of herself as a housewife. In her campaign speeches, she said she thought that govern-ment officials must be honest and trustworthy and that government must not spend more than it earns. People liked that!

The election was held on February 7, 1986. Both Cory and Marcos said they had won. Marcos supporters were accused of using fraud and intimidation in the election. Marcos fled to the United States and died months later in Hawaii.

Cory Aquino was now president of the Philippines and stayed in office for six years. She was noted for her fairness and compassion. The Philippine economy improved. Although others tried to take over the government, she held firm so that a new constitution could take effect. The Filipino people now have more faith in their country and its government.

1. What was there about Cory that made you think she would be a good leader?
2. What facts in the biography suggest that a new government was needed for the Philippines?
3. What things would you want to talk about if Cory came to your class or home?

SOCIAL STUDIES

1. The Philippines are made up of more than seven thousand islands. Which is the largest? Read about the Philippines in a reference book and present three interesting facts about the islands to your class.
2. What sea is west of the Philippines and which one is east?
3. Cory thought of herself as a housewife, yet she was a strong and admired president. What character traits does a person need to lead a country as president?

FURTHER READING

Haskins, James. *Corazon Aquino: Leader of the Philippines*. Hillside, NJ: Enslow Publishers, 1988.

Lepthien, Emilie U. *The Philippines*. Chicago: Childrens Press, 1994.

Philippines in Pictures. Minneapolis, MN: Lerner Publications Company, 1995.

Wheeler, Jill. *Corazon Aquino*. Edina, MN: Abdo & Daughters, 1991.

KEMAL ATATÜRK ★ 1881–1938

Founder and President of the Republic of Turkey

Mustafa Kemal wanted desperately to go to military school, his mother, Zübeyde, preferred that he pursue a religious career. Mustafa's father, Ali Riza, had died when Mustafa was seven years old. Mustafa reminded his mother that his father had hung a sword by his cradle just after his birth. He said defiantly, "I was born to be a soldier. I shall die as a soldier." Zübeyde reluctantly gave in to the twelve-year-old's request.

Mustafa was born in Salonika (now called Thessaloniki), Greece, in the Ottoman Empire. The Ottoman Empire began in the 1300s. In the 1600s, it was the world's largest empire, but during the late 1800s, it was in rapid decline. Its ruler, the Sultan Abdülhamid II, needed a modern army to keep his country together, so the Sultan sent his officers to be trained in other countries. There the men learned what was happening in the rest of the world. A group of the officers called themselves the "Young Turks." Mustafa became one of them.

On one of his assignments, Mustafa had the opportunity to plunder villages for his own personal gain, but he refused. By 1914 Mustafa was a lieutenant colonel, and by 1918 he was a general with much experience and knowledge.

On an assignment to Tripoli, where he and a passenger took a drive in a carriage, some children threw lemon peels at them and mocked them for their fezzes (hats with no brims). The fez allows a Muslim to bow low in prayer and not lose his hat. From that point on, however, Mustafa developed a hatred for the fez and wore the kinds of hats that were popular in the West.

In his travels for the army, he came to believe that women outside the Muslim culture lived a better life. Muslim women were made to wear long, dark dresses, to cover their faces with a veil, and to walk at a respectful distance behind their husbands. They were not to involve themselves in politics. If a Muslim man wanted a divorce, he only had to say, "leave the house" or "I do not want to see you anymore."

In 1923 Mustafa overthrew the Sultan and became the founder and first president of the Republic of Turkey. Now he put into effect the reforms he thought necessary to bring Turkey to the standard of other world powers. He gave women the right to vote. He even encouraged women to dance with men!

Mustafa ordered that all Turks have a family name—that is, a last name, as people in Western cultures had. The Turkish government honored him with the name Atatürk, which means "father of the Turks." Then he was called "Kemal Atatürk." Kemal means "perfection."

Kemal's government created new industries and banks. Education became important. Girls were allowed to attend middle and secondary schools and universities, and soon they entered the professions. Many women stopped wearing the veil because it got in their way at work.

On November 10, 1938, after fifteen years of respected leadership in Turkey, Kemal Atatürk died of a liver problem caused by his heavy drinking.

1. In what ways was Kemal Atatürk like a person you know?
2. List three things Kemal did that you think were important. Share them with a person who did not read the biography.
3. Write a short obituary of Kemal Atatürk in fifty to seventy-five words. Compare yours with a partner's.
4. If you could ask three questions of Kemal, what would they be?

SOCIAL STUDIES

1. What three bodies of water form borders of modern Turkey? Read about modern Turkey in a reference book and give a two-minute talk to your class on some interesting facts you found.
2. With a classmate look in a reference book to find how far the Ottoman Empire extended. Discuss what countries now in existence were formerly controlled by the Ottoman Empire.
3. What religion do Muslims (or Moslems) practice? Who was its founder?

FURTHER READING

Sheehan, Sean. *Turkey*. New York: Marshall Cavendish, 1993.

Tachau, Frank. *Kemal Atatürk*. New York: Chelsea House Publishers, 1988.

Turkey in Pictures. Minneapolis, MN: Lerner Publications Company, 1988.

JOHN JAMES AUDUBON ★ 1785–1851

Naturalist and Painter of North American Birds

John Audobon was born in Haiti and taken to France by his father when he was very young. Everywhere the boy went, he drew birds on his sketch pads. His father, Captain Audubon, had plans for John other than painting pictures of birds. He wanted his son to enter the French navy and go to sea as he had done. But John would not study. For three straight years in the French naval school, he failed to pass any of his exams in mathematics. Captain Audubon gave up and sent John to his Pennsylvania farm in the colonies, where he hoped that John would help run the farm. But John preferred watching and drawing the birds in the surrounding woods.

John loved to watch the phoebes, little birds darting here and there snapping up insects. He followed them to a cave near the farm at Mills Grove. The birds learned to trust him, and some would allow him to pick them up in his hand.

"I wonder if they will come back to this place next year?" John thought. He took some fine silver thread and tied it around one bird's leg. The next year a phoebe came close to John. There it was: a phoebe with a silver thread attached to its leg!

John met a young girl named Lucy Bakewell, who lived on the next farm. She and John fell in love. Lucy's father did not favor the marriage; nor did Captain Audubon. They knew that John was only interested in painting birds. How could he support a wife and family that way? It was true that John was quite careless about almost everything except painting birds. He could paint and draw with either hand.

Then John got his "great idea." He would take his bird paintings to a publisher and have them printed and sold. Lucy agreed to teach school until John had completed his paintings.

No one in the United States would publish his paintings, so John decided to go to England and Scotland to seek a publisher. John traveled throughout England wearing buckskin clothes and smelling of the bear grease he had rubbed on them. He donned a fur trapper's hat and let his beard and hair grow long. People found him delightful and his paintings beautiful, but no one was interested in publishing them.

Then he went to Edinburgh, Scotland, to talk to the printer and engraver William Lizar. He was enthusiastic about John's work. Lizar's engravers etched John's pictures on metal plates. From these metal plates, black-and-white prints were made. Then Lizar's artists colored each print, and the prints were put in portfolios of five apiece. John's job was to sell them. He persuaded wealthy people to buy the portfolios by subscription, just as people now often buy magazines. A set of his prints sold for one thousand dollars. He returned home to Lucy and the boys, but soon he was off to the West to paint the animals of North America.

Today an original set of *The Birds of America* is worth over two million dollars. The oldest and largest conservation organization, the Audubon Society, was founded in 1905 and named for him.

1. Write three things you admired about John Audubon and share them with a partner.
2. If the phoebe John banded with silver thread could talk, what would it say to John when it returned the next year?
3. What reasons do you think John had for traveling through England in buckskin clothes and smelling of bear grease?
4. What is a person called who can use either hand equally well? Do you know a person like this?

SOCIAL STUDIES

1. Go to the library and find some pictures of birds painted by John Audubon. Choose one to learn about. Then draw or paint your own picture of the bird to show to your class.
2. John went to England and Scotland to publish his paintings. Locate these countries on a map. You can find pictures of these countries in travel and reference books at the library.
3. Why do you think an original set of Audubon's bird prints costs so much today?

FURTHER READING

Anderson, Peter. *John James Audubon: Wildlife Artist*. New York: Franklin Watts, 1995.

Kastner, Joseph. *John James Audubon*. New York: Harry N. Abrams, Inc., Publishers, 1992.

Kendall, Martha E. *John James Audubon: Artist of the Wild*. Brookfield, CT: The Millbrook Press, 1993.

ROBERT BADEN-POWELL ★ 1857–1941

Founder of the Boy Scout Movement

His family called him "Stephe" (pronounced Stee-vee) throughout much of his life, but his full name was Robert Stephenson Smyth Baden-Powell. He was born in London, England.

Stephe preferred being outdoors to studying in the classroom. As a result, he did not pass the exam for entering Oxford. Disappointed, he worked hard preparing for the exams necessary to get into the army. Out of 718 who took the examination for the cavalry, Stephe placed second! He found he could do well if he put his mind to it.

Serving in the army gave "Baden," as he was now called, experience among the peoples of India, Afghanistan, and Africa. His first assignment was in Lucknow, India. To get there, he was sent by ship through the Panama Canal and across the Pacific Ocean. He organized the entertainment aboard the ship for the five-week voyage.

His next assignment was in Kandahar, Afghanistan, just northwest of Lucknow. He learned about the capabilities of his men by teaching them tracking and map reading, which other officers did not do. Baden even wrote a book, *Reconnaissance and Scouting,* based on lectures he gave his men.

In 1884 Baden was sent to South Africa to help the British settlers, who were having difficulties with the Boers. The Boers were people of Dutch, French, and German ancestry.

Baden's group was sent to Mafikeng, a small town in Boer territory in the north. Baden's 1,183 men and the African people already in the town were surrounded by the Boers. Baden knew there were Boer spies in the town, so he had his men pretend they were planting mines (explosives) all around the town. Actually, the "mines" were boxes of sand. Then Baden blew up sticks of dynamite as though he were testing the mines. A spy raced out of town on a bicycle to warn the Boers not to attack. The following siege of the town lasted many months, but it kept the Boers from attacking elsewhere. Baden became a hero in England and was given many honors and promoted to major general.

Later, as inspector general of the British Cavalry, he observed a Boys Brigade. Soon he knew that working with young boys was his calling, so Baden retired from the army. His book, *Scouting for Boys,* based on his military experiences, became so successful that Boy Scout troops started up all over the country and in other parts of the world.

The King of England knighted Baden for his work with boys and his heroism at Mafikeng. He was now *Sir* Baden-Powell.

His sister Agnes developed a program for girls called the Girl Guides, and Baden encouraged Juliette Low, a good friend, to begin the Girl Scouts of America in the United States. Soon millions of boys and girls around the world were involved in programs because of Baden's experiences. Baden died in Kenya, Africa, in January of 1941.

1. How do you suppose Baden's ability to draw, paint, and act helped him in his careers as soldier and Boy Scout leader? What abilities do you have that may be helpful to you when you are older?
2. Share with a partner the thing you most admired about Baden in reading his biography.
3. Pretend you are sitting by a campfire in the woods with Baden. What kinds of things would you talk about? Tell him what you know about animals, woods, and camping.

4. The Scout Law has twelve points: to be trustworthy, loyal, helpful, friendly, courteous, kind, obedient, cheerful, thrifty, brave, clean, and reverent. Which three are most important in your mind? Why?

SOCIAL STUDIES

1. Find these places where Baden served Great Britain: Lucknow, India; Kandahar, Afghanistan; and Mafikeng, South Africa. Read about them in a reference book. Which one sounds most interesting to you? Share your reasons with the class.
2. On a globe, trace Baden's trip from England to India through the Panama Canal. What other way could he have gone?
3. Ask a Boy Scout you know (or do it yourself, if you are one) to repeat the Scout Oath and Scout Law in front of the class. Have a discussion on what the Boy Scouts do.

FURTHER READING

Birkby, Robert C. *Boy Scout Handbook*. Irving, TX: Boy Scouts of America, 1992.

Brower, Pauline York. *Baden-Powell: Founder of the Boy Scouts*. Chicago: Childrens Press, 1989.

Fieldbook. Irving, TX: Boy Scouts of America, 1992.

BENJAMIN BANNEKER ★ 1731–1806

Astronomer, Farmer, Mathematician, and Surveyor

enjamin was excited. A package had come from England. His grandmother carefully opened it. "Grandma, what is it?" the five-year-old boy asked. "It's a Bible. I sent for it. Now I can teach you to read!" The first thing she did was to show Benjamin the letter *B* in *Bible*. "See, that letter is the same as the first letter in your name." That was Benjamin's first reading lesson.

A Quaker man started a school near the Bannekers' farm so Benjamin was able to go to school. He was so bright that the teacher soon put him with the older children. In a few years, the teacher told Benjamin there was nothing more he could teach him. He gave Benjamin some of his books to read so he could learn on his own.

One day, when Benjamin was twenty-two, a man loaned him his watch for a week. By candlelight in the evening, Benjamin took the watch apart very carefully and memorized where everything belonged. After a week, he put the watch back together and returned it to its owner in perfect condition. Then Benjamin carved a wooden clock, just like the watch, only larger. He put in a bell to chime the hours. After much work, the clock was completed. For fifty years, it kept time for Benjamin!

In 1759 Benjamin's father died. His sisters had all married and moved away. Benjamin and his mother, now in her sixties, ran the farm. He bought a flute and a violin and learned to play them in the evenings.

When Benjamin was forty years old, the Ellicott family moved nearby. Andrew Ellicott's eighteen-year-old son, George, became Benjamin's friend and loaned him his surveying tools and books on how to survey land. He also loaned him a platform telescope and drafting instruments. Benjamin taught himself to be a surveyor and an astronomer.

With this new knowledge, Benjamin wrote an almanac. Almanacs at that time contained tables that told the rising and setting times of the sun, the moon, and the stars; dates of eclipses; and times of low and high tides. Benjamin made all of the calculations accurately.

In early 1791 President George Washington asked Major Andrew Ellicott IV to head a team surveying the land for the new capital of the United States. Benjamin, now sixty, was chosen to be a part of the team. Secretary of State Thomas Jefferson instructed the team to lay boundaries of the capital in a ten-mile-square pattern. One of Benjamin's chief duties was to keep an astronomical clock so that all measurements for the new national capital were correct. The U.S. government moved from Philadelphia to Washington in 1800.

Benjamin Banneker was one of the first African Americans to be recognized for superior intellectual ability. He is remembered especially for his work on the layout of the boundaries of the District of Columbia.

1. List three personal characteristics Benjamin Banneker had that you think made him successful. Which characteristic would you like to have? Make a plan of things you can do to develop that characteristic in yourself.
2. Discuss and list with a partner the things Benjamin achieved. Which was the most important to you?
3. Look through an almanac. What are the three most interesting things you found in the almanac? Share the information with the class.
4. Pretend you have just entered Benjamin's house as he is studying the watch his friend loaned him. Draw a comic strip showing what Benjamin does with the watch. Add speech and thought bubbles to include what you imagine Benjamin said and thought as he was working.

SOCIAL STUDIES

1. Look in an encyclopedia or other reference book to find the layout of present-day Washington, D.C. What impresses you most about its design? With a small group, make a poster showing the general layout of the U.S. Capital.
2. Of all the historic places in Washington, D.C., which three would be first on your list to visit?
3. Pretend you are having lunch with Benjamin. This is the first time he has been back since 1806. Tell him what has happened in Washington, D.C., and our country. What kind of work can he do now?

FURTHER READING

Altman, Susan. *Extraordinary Black Americans from Colonial to Contemporary Times*. Chicago: Childrens Press, 1989.

Conley, Kevin. *Benjamin Banneker: Scientist and Mathematician*. New York: Chelsea House Publishers, 1989.

Ferris, Jeri. *What Are You Figuring Now? A Story About Benjamin Banneker*. Minneapolis: Carolrhoda Books, Inc., 1988.

Jackson, Garnet Nelson. *Benjamin Banneker: Scientist*. Cleveland, OH: Modern Curriculum Press, 1992.

CLARA BARTON ★ 1821–1912

Founder of the American Red Cross

Early on a Sunday morning, little Clara heard the voices of her two cousins, Jerry and Otis, below her window. "Come ice skating with us!" they called. Immediately, she got into her long petticoat and skirt and stole quietly out the door. The boys took a scarf and tied it around her waist so they could balance her on the ice. Then they tied ice skates to her shoes and off they went, faster and faster. Clara fell and cut her knees badly. The boys tied the scarf around one of the knees to stop the blood and took her home. But Clara's parents had to be told, for the injury was serious. Clara, who was very shy and sorry for sneaking out, later wrote, "I despised myself and failed to sleep or eat" because of the incident.

By the time Clara was three, she could read and write. Her brothers and sisters were much older than she, and each taught her things that interested them. Brother David took her horseback riding. She rode without a saddle, just holding onto the horse's mane. An older brother taught her geography. Yet even with all the help she was given, Clara was constantly afraid she would do something wrong. She was so sensitive that she fainted when she saw workers kill an ox.

Then her brother David fell while building a new barn. Clara spent most of her waking hours in the next two years helping him return to health.

When she was fifteen, Clara started teaching at schools close to her home. Then, in 1850, she went to another town, Bordentown, New Jersey, and started a free school for children. The first day, there were six children. Soon the school blossomed to six hundred. But the officials in the town put a man in charge at twice her salary. She became despondent and went to Washington, D.C. There she became a clerk copyist in the Patent Office, the first woman in history to hold that position.

Several years later, in 1862, during the Civil War, Clara asked for permission to go to the war front to help wounded soldiers. She wrote letters asking for food and bandages and gathered the supplies together to take them to the front. Once, when giving water to a wounded man, a bullet went through her sleeve and into the soldier's chest, killing him.

In 1865 Clara started a project to find men who were missing following the war. Her effort started the Bureau of Records in Washington, D.C.

By 1868, Clara's voice had grown weak and it was necessary for her to rest. She went to Geneva, Switzerland, to recuperate. While she was there, she became interested in the International Red Cross. When she returned to the United States she began a new career as the first president of the American Red Cross.

Clara realized that the Red Cross was needed in peacetime as well as in war. She was able to bring the Red Cross to people who were caught in the Johnstown flood in Pennsylvania in 1889. Thanks to Clara Barton's foresight, the American Red Cross has continued to help those people whose lives are affected by disasters.

1. With a partner, write Clara's first and last name vertically along the left side of a sheet of paper. Use the letters of her name to begin words that describe her (for example: C = courageous).
2. Act out, with three classmates, the time that Clara, Jerry, and Otis stole out of the house to go skating. Don't forget to act out the way Clara returned and confessed. One classmate will need to be Clara's mother.
3. Create a drawing of Clara giving water to a Union soldier during a Civil War battle. Write a caption below the picture.
4. What one thing did Clara do in her life that you wish you could do?

SOCIAL STUDIES

1. Read about the Red Cross in a reference book or go to your local Red Cross office and get material about the Red Cross's functions. Share the information with your classmates.
2. What are the differences among the flags of the three major relief organizations in the world? Draw the flags.
3. How would you feel if you were doing a job well and then someone replaced you and received twice your salary? Is that fair? Why or why not?
4. Read about the Johnstown flood in a reference book. Write a news article about it of less than sixty words. Remember to answer these questions: who? what? when? where? why? and how?

FURTHER READING

Bains, Rae. *Clara Barton: Angel of the Battlefield*. Mahwah, NJ: Troll Communications, 1982.

Dubowski, Cathy East. *Clara Barton: Healing the Wounds*. History of the Civil War Series. Englewood Cliffs, NJ: Silver Burdett Press, 1990.

Hamilton, Leni. *Clara Barton*. New York: Chelsea House Publishers, 1988.

Rose, Mary Catherine. *Clara Barton: Soldier of Mercy*. New York: Chelsea Juniors, 1991.

Sonneborn, Liz. *Clara Barton*. New York: Chelsea Juniors, 1992.

BERNARD MANNES BARUCH 1870–1965

Financier and Statesman

Bernard watched a boy leave his red-and-white peppermint stick in his classroom desk. Candy, especially the kind that was store-bought, was unusual in this poor school. Bernard could not resist. With a friend, he waited until everyone left. Then the two crept under the school, loosened a floor board, climbed into the classroom, and stole the candy. But when he put the candy in his mouth, it tasted bitter. He felt very guilty. Later in life, when he was tempted to do wrong, he remembered that day and it came back to him as a reminder that no true joy or success ever comes without earning it honorably.

When the family moved to New York from South Carolina, Bernard began to learn the value of money. He entered college at the early age of fourteen because he was able to pass the college entrance examination. His father gave him an allowance of twenty-five cents a week plus ten cents a day to take the streetcar for the forty blocks to school. Bernard decided to walk the forty blocks each day so he could save the ten cents.

After college, Bernard's first job paid him three dollars a week. Then he made a great deal of money as a stockbroker on Wall Street in New York City. On the day Bernard became a millionaire, he told his father what he was worth. His father was not impressed and said little, and Bernard began to think seriously about the things that were really important in life.

Because of Bernard's financial brilliance, President Woodrow Wilson asked him to work for the United States government. The president put him in charge of the War Industries Board. This board determined which factories would make uniforms for men in the service, which railroads would carry troops and supplies, and whether steel would go into tanks and guns or into automobiles. Bernard became an unpaid advisor to all the Presidents of the United States from Woodrow Wilson to Dwight D. Eisenhowever. He became known as the "Park Bench Statesman."

In 1942, during World War II, the United States was in a crisis concerning rubber. Rubber was necessary for the tires on trucks and airplanes, but the Japanese had cut off nine-tenths of the natural rubber supply to the United States by occupying the countries that grew rubber for export. Bernard's "Baruch Report" helped the United States solve this dilemma.

After the war Bernard planned, with others, how the United States should *demobilize*—that is, change back to a peacetime economy from wartime productions. Men who fought for their country returned and expected to go back to their former employers or train for other work.

After the war was over, and Bernard was seventy-five years old, he again served his country by becoming the American representative to the United Nations Atomic Energy Commission.

For more than forty years Bernard gave the country the benefit of his experience, intelligence, and integrity. He truly was America's elder statesman.

1. If a parent gave you the choice of using ten cents to take a bus to school or walking and keeping that money, which would you choose? Why? What did you think of Bernard Baruch for choosing to walk? What impressed you most about Bernard?

2. Bernard's mother told him, "Keep your tongue between your teeth unless you have something pleasant to say." What was she trying to tell him? Do you think Bernard followed it? Does your mother, father, or other relative have favorite sayings he or she quotes to you? Write down some of these sayings. See if a classmate can guess what they mean. Then explain them and tell why they are important to you.

3. Pretend you are an adult and your son or daughter comes to you and proudly announces that he or she just became a millionaire. What would you say to him or her?

SOCIAL STUDIES

1. List the presidents of the United States from Wilson through Eisenhower. Ask older relatives or members of a senior citizen organization which president was the best one. Compare their choices.

2. Since the Japanese had cut off all imports of natural rubber to the United States during World War II, what other alternatives were there for getting rubber? (See an encyclopedia reference on Rubber.)

3. What does it mean to be an "elder statesman" or a "Park Bench Statesman"? Write your answer and discuss it with a small group.

FURTHER READING

Cribb, Joe (photography by British Museum and Chas Howson). *Money*. New York: Knopf Books for Young Readers, 1990.

Maestro, Betsy (illustrated by Giulio Maestro). *The Story of Money*. New York: Clarion Books, 1993.

Schwartz, David M. (pictures by Steven Kellogg). *If You Made a Million*. New York: William Morrow & Co., 1994.

Otfinoski, Steve. *The Kid's Guide to Money: Earning It, Saving It, Spending It, Growing It, Sharing It*. New York: Scholastic Inc., 1996.

MARY MCLEOD BETHUNE ★ 1875–1955

Educator

Mary was the fifteenth of seventeen children born to Samuel and Patsy McLeod. She was also the first of the family to be born free, for the Civil War had recently ended. Just ten years before her birth, her mother and father had been slaves, and her older brothers and sisters had been born into slavery.

As a child, however, Mary did not feel completely free, for there was no school for her to attend and she could not read. Indeed, none of her family members could read. In South Carolina at that time, there was no school for African American children.

One day, Emma Wilson came to their door. She told the family that the Presbyterian Mission Board was beginning a school for African American children in Mayesville, five miles away.

Mary walked the five miles to school and back. In the evenings, she taught the rest of the family what she was learning. In a few months, the neighbors brought letters to Mary to read. They also asked for help figuring out how much they should be getting for their cotton crop; some white businessmen did not pay them full price for what they picked.

When she graduated from the Presbyterian Mission School, Mary's thirst for more schooling grew strong. Fortunately, Mary Crissman, a Quaker schoolteacher in Colorado, heard about the mission school. She decided to fund a scholarship for a graduate of the school by doing extra work as a seamstress. Mary was selected for the scholarship.

Mary took her first train ride when traveling to Scotia Seminary for African American girls in Concord, North Carolina. She spent seven years there and did especially well in speech and singing. In 1895 she studied at Moody Bible Institute in Chicago for a year. Mary wanted to be a missionary to Africa, but no openings were available to her.

In the early 1900s, a new railroad was built through Florida. Wealthy white people went there to spend vacation time, and many African American laborers went there with their families to find work. Mary chose Daytona Beach to begin her school, for there were crowded labor camps and no schools for laborers' children. She arrived in Daytona Beach with her son Albert, where she found an old cottage to rent as a school. Then she bicycled around telling people of the new school, the Daytona Normal and Industrial School for Girls.

Whites and African Americans became interested and supported her financially. It grew into a junior high school, then a high school, and then a college. Because there was no hospital for African Americans, she established one herself. After starting out with only two beds, it grew to a twenty-bed hospital. In 1925 the college merged with an all-boys school and became Bethune-Cookman College, a four-year co-educational college with Mary as its first president

Bethune-Cookman College now serves a predominately African American student body on a fifty-two-acre urban campus. Students earn bachelor's degrees in business, education, the humanities, science, mathematics, and the social sciences.

1. With a partner, write a song about Mary McLeod Bethune. Sing it to your class-mates. Be sure to include five interesting facts about her life.
2. Make a list of things that would not have happened if Mary Crissman had not taken on extra work as a seamstress to pay for Mary's tuition to Scotia Seminary.

3. You have just been invited to the campus of Bethune-Cookman College. Mary invites you into her office. She tells you that you can ask her any questions you wish to ask. What will you ask her?

SOCIAL STUDIES

1. Bethune-Cookman College is in Daytona Beach, Florida. Find Daytona Beach on a map. Then go to the library to find the address of the college. As a class, write to Bethune-Cookman for a brochure and other information about the school.
2. Talk to several adults about charities they support, as Mary Crissman did. Report to your class how these charities help people. What kinds of charities will you support when you are older?

3. You are going to start your own school. Write a page describing the school. What kinds of students can attend? Where is it located? What are its educational goals?

FURTHER READING

Greenfield, Eloise. *Mary McLeod Bethune*. New York: HarperCollins Children's Books, 1994.

Meltzer, Milton. *Mary McLeod Bethune: Voice of Black Hope*. Women of Our Time Series. New York: Puffin Books, 1988.

McKissack, Patricia and Fred. *Mary Mcleod Bethune*. Cornerstones of Freedom Series. Chicago, IL: Childrens Press, 1992.

Turner, Glennette Tilley. *Take a Walk in Their Shoes*. New York: Puffin Books, 1992.

ELIZABETH BLACKWELL ★ 1821–1910

Physician

Elizabeth Blackwell's father, Samuel Blackwell, had a prosperous sugar refining company in England. As an abolitionist, he was troubled that he had to accept raw sugar cane cut by Caribbean slave labor. When his sugar business verged on bankruptcy, Samuel called his family together and told them his plans: They would start anew in the American colonies. Soon after, unfortunately, he died, and the family was left with twenty dollars and many bills.

Elizabeth's mother started a school, and her daughters became the teachers. The boys, who were younger, did other jobs, and the family managed to survive and stay together. Elizabeth, the third child, was much like her father in concern for others. One day, as she sat with an older woman who was dying, the woman asked Elizabeth why she did not study medicine. "Oh, no," she said, "I get sick just thinking about what doctors must do."

The thought of becoming a doctor would not leave her, however, for she wanted to do something with her life that would make a difference. Her first step was to study with a doctor in Asheville, North Carolina. He helped her prepare for entering medical school. While in North Carolina, she taught school to support herself. When she applied to twenty-eight medical schools, she received only rejections. Some would not even reply. It was unheard-of for a woman to want to be a doctor.

But a strange thing happened when she applied to Geneva College in upper New York state. In her application, she included a letter of recommendation from a doctor friend whom the administrators and faculty at Geneva knew. Not wanting to offend the man, the faculty decided to let the students, all men, vote on whether to accept a woman as a member of the student body. The faculty hoped the students would reject Elizabeth. Yet the students took the voting as a joke, and every one of them voted to accept her!

Not everyone was happy to have Elizabeth at the school or in the community, but she worked hard and graduated at the top of her class. Finding a place to gain her practical experience was another matter. She finally went to Paris and interned at a woman's hospital. In caring for a child, she contracted a serious eye infection. She lost the sight in her left eye and then needed a glass eye replacement. This misfortune prevented Elizabeth from pursuing her goal of becoming a surgeon.

She returned to the United States and opened a clinic for poor women and children. Elizabeth believed very strongly that sanitation and personal cleanliness were extremely important if diseases were to be prevented.

When the Civil War began, Elizabeth organized the nursing service for the Union forces. After the war, she opened Women's Medical College in New York City, which was the first institution of its kind in history.

The American Medical Women's Association established a medal in her honor: The Elizabeth Blackwell Medal. It is awarded yearly to a woman who makes important contributions that advance women's role in medicine.

1. List three titles you would give to Elizabeth Blackwell's biography.
2. What personal characteristics do you think Elizabeth inherited from her mother? Her father?
3. Pretend you are a friend sitting with Elizabeth as she opens the letters of rejection from the twenty-eight medical schools. What does she say? What do you say to her? Try role-playing this scene with a partner.

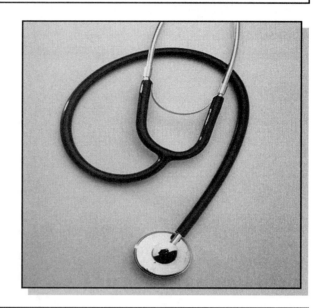

SOCIAL STUDIES

1. In what mountain range is Asheville, North Carolina, located? Read about Asheville, North Carolina, in a reference book and report to your class three items that interest you about the area.
2. Take a survey of the students in your class. Ask how many have a family doctor as their physician. Then determine how many of the physicians are female and how many are male. What does your study tell you?
3. Write a page on why you would or would not want to be a physician.

FURTHER READING

Brown, Jordan. *Elizabeth Blackwell.* American Women of Achievement Series. New York: Chelsea House Publishers, 1989.

Curtis, Robert H. Medicine: *Great Lives.* Great Lives Series. New York: Simon & Schuster, 1993.

Latham, Jean Lee. *Elizabeth Blackwell: Pioneer Woman Doctor.* Discovery Biographies. New York: Chelsea Juniors, 1991.

Sabin, Francene. *Elizabeth Blackwell: The First Woman Doctor.* Mahwah, NJ: Troll Communications, 1982.

Schleichert, Elizabeth. *The Life Of Elizabeth Blackwell.* Pioneers in Health and Medicine Series. Frederick, MD: Twenty-First Century Books, 1991.

NELLIE BLY (Elizabeth Cochrane Seaman) ★ 1867–1922

Journalist

She was Elizabeth Cochran, but as a teenager she thought Cochran was not quite right, so she added an *e*. How she became Nellie Bly is a longer story.

Elizabeth's father, Michael Cochran, could rarely sit still. He became a justice of the peace, a judge, a store owner, a post office manager, and an owner of a grist mill. Michael had ten children by his first wife. When she died, he remarried and had five more children, one of whom was Elizabeth. In a family of mostly boys, Elizabeth had to fight for recognition, which she learned to do quite well.

A career was what Elizabeth wanted. In the late 1800s, about the only careers for women were teaching, nursing, and working as a governess. None of these interested her. Then one day she read an editorial in the *Pittsburgh Dispatch*. The author wrote that young women should be satisfied with marriage and a family rather than a career. She sent off an angry letter to the editor, who ended up offering Elizabeth a job on the newspaper and giving her the pen name "Nelly Bly" (after a popular Stephen Foster song). The typesetter wrote *Nellie* with the letters *ie* and it was never changed.

Her first article, "Mad Marriages," was on the subject of divorce. Everyone wondered who wrote the article. Many thought it was a man. From that point, Elizabeth wrote about the dangerous conditions women had to endure working in factories that produced cigars, shoes, bread, pickles, relishes, and other products. They had to work twelve to fourteen hours a day for very low wages.

Often Nellie would take a job in these places to get the feel of what women, men, and some young children endured.

The *Dispatch* sent her to Mexico to write about conditions there. Her mother went with her on the train. In Mexico, she found the plight of the workers even worse than in the United States. On the trip, she saw men sitting back and smoking, while their wives did the hard manual labor. Her articles were very critical of these conditions.

In 1887 Nellie went to New York to work for publisher Joseph Pulitzer at the *New York World*. She got the job after pretending insanity in order to learn about conditions in an infamous mental asylum on Blackwell's Island. First, she fooled the police into taking her to a public hospital for the mentally disturbed. Then a judge transferred her to the asylum. There she found abused patients, many of whom were only frightened or did not speak English. Her newspaper articles on this experience began the needed reforms.

In 1890 she traveled around the world in the record-breaking time of seventy-two days, six hours, and eleven minutes, traveling on ships, trains, donkeys, and even a *jinrikisha*. She broke the fictional record of the character, Phineas Fogg, in Jules Vernes' novel *Around the World in Eighty Days*, with time to spare.

She married American businessman Robert Seaman in 1895 and became Elizabeth Cochrane Seaman. But newspaper readers knew her as Nellie Bly, reporter.

1. Would you choose Nellie Bly as an older sister? Why or why not? If so, what would you do together?
2. Does Nellie Bly remind you of anyone you know? Who? In what way?
3. Write a brief newspaper obituary summarizing the life of Nellie Bly.
4. Write a letter to the editor of the *Pittsburgh Dispatch,* just as Nellie did, stating your opinion on whether women should be satisfied with marriage and family instead of a career.

SOCIAL STUDIES

1. With your finger on a map, trace where Nellie and her mother might have traveled by train from St. Louis to Mexico. Read about Mexico and tell your class what most interests you about the country.
2. Plan a flying trip around the world from Chicago. Stop on every continent except Antarctica. List the cities and countries where you land and take off and what you might see in each place.
3. What is a *jinrikisha?* Read about them in a reference book. Draw a picture of one and show it to a friend or parent.
4. Pretend you are a journalist for your local newspaper. What pen name would you give yourself? Make a list of five subjects you would like to investigate and write about.

FURTHER READING

Ehrlich, Elizabeth. *Nellie Bly.* American Women of Achievement Series. New York: Chelsea House Publishers, 1989.

Gibbons, Gail. *Deadline! From News to Newspaper.* New York: HarperCollins Children's Books, 1987.

Granfield, Linda. *Extra! Extra! The Who, What, Where, When and Why of Newspapers.* New York: Orchard Books, 1994.

Quackenbush, Robert. *Stop the Presses, Nellie's Got a Scoop! A Story of Nellie Bly.* New York: Simon & Schuster Children's Books, 1992.

SIMÓN BOLÍVAR   ★ 1780–1830

Military Leader and Liberator

Simón José Antonio de la Santísima Trinidad Bolívar y Palacios was his full name. The people of South America knew him as "Simón Bolívar." He was the fourth child of a wealthy family in Caracas, Venezuela. His father died when he was three, and a black female slave named Hippolyta was mainly responsible for raising him. He later remarked that, "I never knew any father but her." When Hippolyta grew older, Simón made sure that she had a pension to live on for the rest of her life.

When Simón was fifteen, his mother died. Even at this young age, he was a second lieutenant in the militia, in which his father had been a colonel.

During these early years, his tutor, Simón "Robinson" Rodríguez, used the classics and the novel *Robinson Crusoe* to teach Simón. Rodríguez was so enchanted by the adventure story of Robinson Crusoe that he, himself, preferred to be called "Robinson." Robinson Rodríguez's theory of educating Simón came from the French philosopher Jean-Jacques Rousseau. Rousseau taught that a teacher must attract a child's interests rather than use tiresome drills. Robinson also made sure that Simón developed into an excellent horseman, swimmer, and hiker. Later, Simón learned to speak fluent French. When he was older, he commented that never a day went by that he did not read.

His uncle, now his guardian, sent Simón to Madrid, Spain, to live with his mother's brother. There, at seventeen, he fell deeply in love with María Teresa, who was even younger than he

was. They were married and sailed to Caracas. But ten months after they settled down, María Teresa died of yellow fever. Simón was devastated and swore he would never marry again.

The American Revolution, the war that abolished Great Britain's rule over the American colonies, influenced Simón greatly. Spain ruled over much of South America in much the same way that Great Britain had controlled the colonies. Simón felt that Venezuela must become a free country of its own too.

Simón spent time in Europe mingling with people who shared his views and who were excited about freedom and democracy. Eventually, he vowed to fight until Venezuela was free, a country on its own and out from under Spain's influence. He returned to Venezuela and formed his army with six hundred patriots. In effect, Simón Bolívar declared war on the vast Spanish Empire.

In 1823 Simón led an army of Colombians and Venezuelans into Peru to help other South Americans who wanted the Spanish driven from the continent. This was accomplished in 1826. Because of Simón's leadership, part of Peru became a country of its own and was named Bolivia, and in Venezuela, dollars are called Bolívars.

In 1830 Simón resigned as president of Colombia and died that same year. In his farewell, he said, "You should all labor for the boundless benefit of the Union. My last wishes are for the happiness of our homeland." Simón Bolívar will always be remembered as the great *Libertador*.

1. List three things in Simón Bolívar's education that helped him in his career as a military leader. What are you learning that might help you to become a leader?
2. What might have happened if Simón had settled in Madrid, Spain, and not returned to Venezuela?
3. With a partner, role-play a conversation between Hippolyta as an elderly black slave and Simón Bolívar as the little boy she cared for who is now a dashing Venezuelan general.

4. Discuss the meaning of Simón's statement, "You should all labor for the boundless benefit of the Union."

SOCIAL STUDIES

1. On a map or globe find these places known to Simón Bolívar in South America: Caracas, Venezuela; Bogatá, Colombia; Valencia, Venezuela; Ecuador; Peru; Bolivia; and Panama. With a small group select one of these places to learn more about and report on to your class.
2. In a reference book, find a map of the areas of South America that were part of the Spanish Empire when Simón began fighting. Trace the continent on paper and use markers to outline the countries under Spanish control.

3. In what ways were the American Revolution and the Venezuelan Revolution similar?

FURTHER READING

Adler, David A. *Picture Book of Simón Bolivar*. New York: Holiday House, 1992.

de Varona, Frank. *Simón Bolivar: Latin American Liberator*. Hispanic Heritage Series. Brookfield, CT: The Millbrook Press, 1993.

Jacobs, William Jay. *World Government*. Great Lives Series. New York: Simon & Schuster Children's Books, 1993.

LOUIS BRAILLE ★ 1809–1852

Inventor of Printing and Writing for the Visually Impaired

In the little village of Coupvray, just west of Paris, three-year-old Louis Braille walked into his father's harness shop. He saw a piece of leather and tools on a table. Imitating his father, he climbed on a work bench and pretended to manipulate the tools. Carefully, he picked up an awl—a pointed metal object—and began stabbing it into the leather before him. By accident, it entered his left eye. His parents heard him scream and ran to find him.

There was nothing they could do but wash him off and call for a local woman to help. She administered a poultice of herbs and recommended changing bandages. At that time, there were no antibiotics to stop infection. Within a few days, the infection passed over to his other eye and he went blind in both.

A young priest, Jacques Palluy, was assigned to the parish where the Brailles lived. He took an interest in Louis and three times a week gave him instruction in Bible, literature, and poetry. Now six years old, Louis did extremely well, and the priest encouraged the local teacher to accept Louis in the village school. Soon Louis was doing difficult mathematical problems in his head before the older students could work them out on paper. In history class, he could recite yesterday's lesson exactly as he heard it. But there were no books for a visually impaired boy like Louis to read!

In 1819, when he was ten, Louis had the opportunity to attend the Royal Institute for Blind Youth in Paris. His father was reluctant to let him go, for Louis would only be able to come home at vacation times; the school was four hours by stagecoach from his little village.

At the Royal Institute he took classes in history, grammar, mathematics, Latin, and geography. He excelled in all of his subjects. He even had music classes and learned to play the cello, piano, and organ. To help with the expenses of the school, the students made crafts to sell. Louis made excellent slippers.

A retired artillery captain from the French army came to the school and demonstrated a method used by soldiers to send messages at night. By punching holes in paper, men could touch the raised dots and read messages without seeing them. Louis became excited with the idea and simplified the system by using fewer raised dots. By the time he was fifteen, Louis had developed a plan of writing that became known as *braille*.

When he was nineteen, Louis became a teacher at the school and invented a raised dot system for music as well. He played the organ on Sundays for churches. At twenty-six he discovered that he had tuberculosis, a fatal disease. The school in which he had lived since he was ten was so musty and damp that he and other students contracted the disease.

Yet Louis kept working and finally invented a machine that typed alphabet letters from raised braille dots. With another man, he developed the braille printing press. Then, just two days before his forty-third birthday, Louis Braille passed away. He left inventions that have helped millions of visually impaired children and adults around the world to become productive citizens.

1. What did you feel as you read about Louis Braille? Compare your feelings and responses with a partner's.
2. In your mind, what was Louis's most admirable personality trait? What is your strongest personality trait?
3. How does any physical challenge you may have compare to that of Louis's?
4. Pretend you are sitting with Louis as he plays the piano or cello. What would you talk about? What questions would you ask?

SOCIAL STUDIES

1. Invite a special-needs teacher or other knowledgeable adult to your class to talk about how one can best serve and treat people with physical challenges.
2. The terms *blind* and *visually impaired* are often used to mean the same thing. List some specific things you and a friend might do to help the visually impaired people you meet.
3. With a relative or friend, count the number of steps going up or down in your home or school. Try walking slowly up and down the steps with your eyes closed to get the feeling of a visual handicap. Make sure someone is nearby to help if you experience difficulty.
4. Look up the braille alphabet in a reference book. With a pin or other sharp instrument, create a message to exchange with a classmate.

FURTHER READING

Birch, Beverley. *Louis Braille*. People Who Have Helped the World. Milwaukee, WI: Gareth Stevens Children's Books, 1989.

Bryant, Jennifer Fisher. *Louis Braille*. Great Achievers. New York: Chelsea House Publishers, 1994.

Davidson, Margaret. *Louis Braille: The Boy Who Invented Books for the Blind*. New York: Scholastic, 1991.

Lantier, Patricia, and Beverley Birch. *Louis Braille*. People Who Made a Difference Series. Milwaukee, WI: Gareth Stevens Children's Books, 1991.

WILLIAM JENNINGS BRYAN 1860–1925

Orator and Statesman

William worked hard on his father's Illinois farm by gathering hay, digging post holes, milking cows, caring for livestock, and cutting timber. He grew up physically strong as well as solid in his Christian beliefs.

The three main churches in the nearby town were Baptist, Methodist, and Presbyterian. Because his father was Baptist, William went to the Baptist church for morning Sunday school. His mother was Methodist, so he also went to the Methodist Sunday school later in the day. When he was fourteen, William committed himself to the Christian faith and joined the Presbyterian church for the rest of his life.

A few years after joining the church, he met Mary Baird. Her friends told her they thought William was "too good" because he didn't smoke, drink, curse, or dance. Mary thought about that and decided since she did none of these things, she would go out with him. To her, it was better to have a man "too good" than "not good enough." After William finished law school and started his law practice, he and Mary were married.

William and Mary settled in the town of Jacksonville, Illinois, in 1883, but he found it difficult to make a living as a lawyer in such a small town. One month, he only made $2.50. So when a friend from law school invited him to come to Lincoln, Nebraska, to join him in setting up a law firm, he decided to go.

One of his first jobs was to collect debts from people who did not pay for their drinks at a local saloon. This caused William a bit of a dilemma, for he was against drinking alcoholic beverages and also against owing money and not paying debts. He took the job, but he told the saloon owner that he was against the sale of liquor.

In 1890 he won a seat in the United States Congress. At the Democratic National Convention in Chicago in 1896, William made a dramatic speech titled the "Cross of Gold," in which he urged the free coinage of silver. At thirty-six, he became the Democratic nominee for president. William was the first presidential candidate to travel by railroad to speak to the people. But his efforts were in vain, for he lost presidential elections to William McKinley in 1896 and 1900 and to William Howard Taft in 1909. Later, he served as President Wilson's secretary of state.

William was a religious fundamentalist who believed in a literal interpretation of the Bible. He defended this view, and opposed the teaching of evolution in public schools, in the famous Scopes "Monkey Trial." William won.

Between 1894 and 1924, William gave nearly five thousand lectures. People came great distances to hear him speak, even those who disagreed with him on issues or along party lines. The people nicknamed him the Great Commoner because he championed popular causes.

What William proposed and worked for, presidents were able to carry out. He advocated reforms in the federal income tax, women's right to vote, stricter railroad regulation, and publicizing campaign contributions.

1. What did you most admire about William Jennings Bryan? If you were to write a book about him, what title would you give it?
2. Would you rather have a husband or wife that was "too good" or "not good enough"? Explain.
3. What do William's three attempts to become president of the United States tell you about his character as a person?
4. William did not put a high priority on making money. On a scale of one to ten, how important is making money to you? Compare your rating with those of a small group of classmates and discuss.

SOCIAL STUDIES

1. Look up the Scopes Trial in a reference book and read about it. Arrange a class debate, with one side arguing that schools should teach evolution and the other side arguing that schools should teach the Bible's version of creation.
2. What beliefs do you have that are different from those of most of your friends? Do others ever challenge your beliefs? How do you react?
3. William was probably best known for his speeches. Write and give a short speech on something about which you feel strongly.

4. Would a person like William make a good candidate for president of the United States in the next national election? Why or why not? Read the biography to your parents and ask them this question.

FURTHER READING

Allen, Robert. *William Jennings Bryan*. Milford, MI: Mott Media, 1992.

Blake, Arthur. *The Scopes Trial: Defending the Right to Teach*. Spotlight on American History Series. Brookfield, CT: The Millbrook Press, 1994.

KIT CARSON ★ 1809–1868

Frontiersman

His given name was Christopher, but everyone called him "Kit." The year after Kit was born in Kentucky, the family moved to Boon's Lick, Missouri. He was one of fourteen children. His father wanted him to become a lawyer, but when Kit was nine years old, his father was killed by a falling tree.

Kit was apprenticed at fourteen to David Workman's saddle shop. Here he heard about mountain men who trapped animals for their fur high in the mountains of the West. By sixteen, Kit had had enough of making saddles and headed west without a word. Workman put a notice in the paper offering one cent to the person bringing the boy back to him.

Kit spent his first year in the western mountains trapping with a mountain man who taught him to speak Spanish. Later, Kit was hired to cook for a party of trappers. His boss, the trappers, and even poor Kit could not eat his first meal, but eventually he mastered cooking.

Kit also learned how to live with as well as fight against Native Americans. The Native Americans often ran off with horses owned by settlers, mountain men, and army troops. Kit excelled as a tracker of Native Americans and as a fur trapper.

Kit met a beautiful Native American girl. Her name was Waanibe, or Grass Singing, but Kit called her Alice. A very strong Frenchman, Captain Drips, was also interested in her. In a drunken rage, Drips beat up several men. Kit, although much smaller, challenged Drips. They rode their horses close to each other; Drips's bullet grazed Kit's hair and powder burned one of his eyes for a moment, but Kit's bullet went through Drips's arm. Drips never bothered Kit after that.

Kit married Waanibe, and they had a little girl whom Kit called Adeline. But Kit was always traveling and there was little time to spend with her. When Waanibe died a short time later, Kit took Adeline to his sister in Missouri to be raised.

After settling Adeline with his sister, Kit met a Lieutenant Frémont on a steamer. Frémont was preparing to explore the West. The Lieutenant hired Kit as his guide throughout the West, and together they had many adventures. The eastern newspapers learned of the two men, and Kit became known as the "Hero of the Plains."

Kit decided to settle down. He married Josefa Jaramillo of Taos, New Mexico, and Taos became his home.

When the war with Mexico broke out in 1846, Kit guided General Stephen W. Kearney to California. Kearney's troops were attacked by Mexican forces at San Pasqual, California, near Escondido. Kit and two others were able to sneak through the Mexican lines to get help in San Diego. They lost their shoes but walked and crawled through cactus and over stones for thirty miles to save Kearney's troops.

During the Civil War, Kit fought Confederate forces at the battle of Valverde, New Mexico, near Socorro. Kit Carson, a hunter, guide, and soldier, is remembered as a legendary frontiersman who was at home in the "wild, wild West."

1. What would make you think that David Workman was not really interested in having Kit Carson come back as an apprentice saddle maker? What do you suppose Workman said to his close friends about Kit's departure?
2. Kit and two others walked and crawled for thirty miles to get help for their army unit in California. What place do you go to from time to time that is at least thirty miles from where you live? Write a sentence or two telling what you think of Kit and his friends for accomplishing such a feat.
3. Choose an incident from Kit's biography and draw a cartoon showing what happened.
4. Make up three titles for Kit's biography.

SOCIAL STUDIES

1. Kit called Taos, New Mexico, home. Which direction from Taos is Sante Fe? Trace your finger on a map or globe from St. Louis, Missouri, to Taos, New Mexico, to Santa Fe, New Mexico, to Escondido, California, back to San Diego, California, back to Valverde (Socorro), New Mexico, and then back to Taos, New Mexico. Read about Taos in a reference book, and share three interesting facts with the class. As a class, write to the Taos tourist information office and request information on Taos and Kit Carson's home.
2. What does it mean to be an apprentice? Look up the word in a dictionary. If you could be an apprentice in any area or career, what would it be?
3. Few Civil War battles were fought in the southwestern United States. Where were they most often fought?
4. With a small group, read about fur trapping in a reference book and discuss what you found. In your opinion, what fur is the most beautiful? Should people wear fur hats and coats nowadays?

FURTHER READING

Gleiter, Jan, and Kathleen Thompson. *Kit Carson*. First Biographies Series. Austin, TX: Raintree Steck-Vaughn, 1995.

Sanford, William R. *Kit Carson: Frontier Scout*. Springfield, NJ: Enslow Publishers, 1996.

Zandra, Dan. *Kit Carson: Trailblazer of the West (1809–1868)*. We the People Series. Mankato, MN: Creative Education, 1988.

RACHEL CARSON 1907–1964

Marine Biologist and Science Writer

Rachel loved to read and to write. During World War I, she wrote a story for *St. Nicholas*, a children's magazine with a section that was reserved for writing submitted by children. Rachel's story was titled "A Battle in the Clouds." It was based on a letter her older brother had sent to the family from the air base where he was stationed in Europe. When her story was accepted, Rachel received a Silver Badge award, and the editor paid her ten dollars. At the age of ten, Rachel was a published and paid writer.

During her high school years, she wrote for the school newspaper and decided to major in literature in college. Then she took a required course in biology with Mary Skinker as her instructor. The study of plants and animals, and the excitement her teacher brought to class about them, changed Rachel's mind.

Jobs in the sciences were open only to men. A scholarship in zoology at Johns Hopkins University helped her obtain a master's degree. She studied during the summer at the prestigious Woods Hole Marine Biological Laboratory on the coast of Massachusetts, and there she had her first contact with the ocean.

The professional break she needed as a science writer came when the *Baltimore Sunday Sun* published her articles on fisheries. Rachel submitted an article on the sea to the *Atlantic Monthly*, a national magazine. One person who read the article was a book publisher. He wrote Rachel and asked her to write a book for his company. The book, *Under the Sea Wind*, established her as an excellent writer and a

meticulous scientist. Her next book, *The Sea Around Us*, became a best-seller.

Rachel became well known as a marine biologist and science writer. This led to her receiving a number of honorary doctoral degrees, speaking engagements, and the National Book Award.

As most people do, Rachel experienced difficult times. Close family members died, and Rachel adopted a nephew and raised him herself. She also cared for her elderly mother. Then Rachel was diagnosed with cancer.

Through all of these difficulties, Rachel kept writing, studying, and publishing. Her biggest project lay before her. In the 1950s, the government under President Eisenhower became less concerned with protecting our natural resources and more interested in promoting large industries. Lumber companies cut down forests extensively, chemical companies produced pesticides without adequate knowledge of their danger to the environment, and atomic-energy use and testing released radioactive substances into the food chain. The pesticide DDT was especially deadly. It was used to destroy insects in fields, but it also killed birds in surrounding areas.

Rachel wrote a book, *Silent Spring*, that warned people what was happening to our earth. Farmers, the chemical industry, agricultural groups, and even the medical profession criticized her. But the public realized that she was correct. Death silenced Rachel in 1964, yet her books live on.

1. Pretend you are Rachel. Write five short sentences, beginning each sentence with the word *I*.
2. Rachel Carson was a meticulous scientist. What does it mean to be meticulous? Who do you know that is meticulous?
3. Write a sentence stating what you most admired about Rachel. Read your sentence to a small group of classmates.
4. If you were to write a story for a children's magazine, what do you think you would write about?

SOCIAL STUDIES

1. What area of science is most interesting to you? How did you come to be interested in it?
2. Find one of Rachel's books at the library. Choose three interesting things she says and share them with the class.
3. If Rachel were still alive, what would concern her about today's environment? What concerns you about the environment?
4. With a small group, choose an environmental issue. Brainstorm things you can do to help. Make a poster sharing your tips with the class.

FURTHER READING

Foster, Leila M. *The Story of Rachel Carson and the Environmental Movement*. Cornerstones of Freedom Series. Chicago, IL: Childrens Press, 1990.

Jezer, Marty. *Rachel Carson*. American Women of Achievement Series. New York: Chelsea House Publishers, 1988.

Ransom, Candice F. *Listening to Crickets: A Story About Rachel Carson*. Minneapolis, MN: Carolrhoda Books, Inc., 1993.

Stille, Darlene R. *Extraordinary Women Scientists*. Chicago, IL: Childrens Press, 1995.

Wadsworth, Ginger. *Rachel Carson: Voice for the Earth*. Minneapolis, MN: Lerner Group, 1992.

GEORGE WASHINGTON CARVER ★ 1864–1943

Agricultural Research Scientist and Teacher

Moses and Susan Carver, who were white, did not believe in purchasing people as slaves. But their farm was too large to handle by themselves, and there was no other help available. So Moses bought a young slave named Mary to keep his wife company and help tend the farm. Mary got married and had two children. The older boy, James, was strong and a great help around the farm. The baby, George, was sickly.

When he was eight years old, George talked to a friend who told him about Sunday school and prayer. That afternoon George tried saying a prayer. Later he told people that "God just came into my heart." When George grew up, he used prayer as inspiration in his work.

George loved nature. He wanted to know the name of everything he found in the woods. For years, he tried to get an education. He went away and worked for people who lived near a school that would allow him in class. Along this journey, he learned to read, write, and do arithmetic. He also learned to paint, sing, and do laundry. Doing laundry for other people gave George money to live on and attend school. By 1894, he received a bachelor of science degree in agriculture from the college that later became Iowa State University. Then he earned his master's degree and became a teacher at the school.

Booker T. Washington asked George to come to Alabama to teach African American students at Tuskegee. Washington was head of the African American school that in 1985 became Tuskegee University. George accepted the offer and took on several responsibilities besides teaching students.

George took his students directly into the fields to teach them how to enrich the soil in cotton fields. Cotton depleted the ground of its nutrients because farmers raised the crop on the same fields year after year. He taught his students how to rotate crops, showing them how raising cowpeas, soybeans, sweet potatoes, and peanuts would put nutrients back into the soil.

George also worked in his laboratory, experimenting with ways to develop other uses for sweet potatoes, peanuts, and other crops. He wrote his findings in easily understood English and published them in booklets for farmers and others to read.

George practiced what he called "creative chemistry." He discovered that he could make more than 150 products from the sweet potato. These products included library paste, medicine, and paints and dyes.

George was most successful with the peanut. He made more than 300 products from peanuts: candy bars, cereal, a milk substitute, dye, glue, face powder, printer's ink, salad oil, soap, nitroglycerine, and instant coffee, to name a few. His agricultural research brought him international recognition and an offer of $100,000 a year to work in Thomas Edison's laboratory, which he turned down.

George died in 1943. On his tombstone is this inscription: "He could have added fortune to fame, but caring for neither, he found happiness and honor in being helpful to the world."

1. What meanings does the epitaph on George's tombstone have for you? Copy it slowly and think about it. What would you like to have written on your tombstone?
2. How could George have accumulated a large fortune if he had desired to do so?

3. Pretend you are walking in the fields at Tuskegee with George. What does he tell you about his preference for teaching young African American students instead of doing other things with his life?

SOCIAL STUDIES

1. Read books and references about George's investigations of peanuts. Make a list of his five most interesting discoveries. Compare them with lists made by your classmates.
2. For what reason would you call George an "environmentalist" rather than an "inventor"?
3. George practiced "creative chemistry" and produced many things from peanuts and other foods. Why do you think such research was important? If George were alive today, how do you think he would use his "creative chemistry"?

FURTHER READING

Adair, Gene. *George Washington Carver: Botanist*. Black Americans of Achievement Series. New York: Chelsea House Publishers, 1989.

Aliki. *A Weed Is a Flower: The Life of George Washington Carver*. New York: Simon & Schuster Children's Books, 1988.

Altman, Susan. *Extraordinary Black Americans from Colonial to Contemporary Times*. Chicago: Childrens Press, 1989.

Gray, James Marion. *George Washington Carver*. Pioneers in Change Series. Englewood Cliffs, NJ: Silver Burdett Press, 1990.

Greene Carol. *George Washington Carver: Scientist and Teacher*. Rookie Biography Series. Chicago, IL: Childrens Press, 1992.

Mitchell, Barbara. *A Pocketful of Goobers: A Story About George Washington Carver*. Minneapolis, MN: Carolrhoda Books, Inc., 1986.

Rogers, Teresa. *George Washington Carver: Nature's Trailblazer*. Earthkeepers Series. Frederick, MD: Twenty-First Century Books, 1992.

MARY CASSATT ★ 1844–1926

Impressionist Painter

In the 1800s women painted pictures but did not make painting a career. Most art schools only admitted men. But Mary Cassatt set her heart on becoming a professional artist. In many ways, she was much like her father—very stubborn. At twenty-one she told her father of her decision and he bellowed, "I would almost rather see you dead!" But Mary did not waver.

In 1866 she arrived at France's most distinguished art academy, the École des Beaux-Arts, only to find that they did not take women! Although she was angry, her stubborn streak arose in her. She found a famous art teacher, who gave her private lessons. Then she went to the Louvre, a large museum with many priceless paintings, and practiced making copies of the paintings.

To be accepted as a painter in France, artists submitted their work to the Salon in Paris. The judges, who were older men, decided which pictures to show. Out of 5,000 entries only 2,500 were accepted. Mary had a painting accepted. It was *The Mandolin Player*, a picture of a young girl playing the mandolin. Even though the painting did not sell, she was pleased. Then her parents called her home because the French Emperor, Napoleon III, declared war on Prussia, a part of Germany. France lost the war and Paris was in ruins.

Mary continued painting at home. She sent some of her paintings to a Chicago art dealer, who tried to sell them but soon after the paintings reached Chicago, the Great Chicago Fire of 1871 burned the building where they

were stored. Following this disaster, a Catholic bishop in Pittsburgh paid her to go to Parma, Italy, to make copies of two religious paintings by the painter Correggio. Then she went to Spain, where she created the painting *Torero and Young Girl*. The painting was selected for showing in the Salon in 1873.

At that time a group of artists in Paris were experimenting with new art techniques. They were not happy with the judging at the Salon. These artists, called *impressionists*, used bolder colors and freer strokes than traditional artists. The Salon judges thought their work was too modern.

Mary was forced to make a decision. If she painted the way the judges in the Salon wanted, she could continue to sell her paintings. But she decided to paint the way she wanted. One of her impressionist paintings was *A Little Girl in a Blue Armchair*. In the painting the little girl slumps in her chair. She is not stiff and lifeless like the subjects in many portraits that the Salon painters painted.

Mary became known for her lifelike paintings of babies and children. She chose plain children as her models. Her young model in *Girl Arranging Her Hair* is a good example: she is ordinary and therefore more realistic.

The French gave Mary their Legion of Honor award for her work, and her school in Philadelphia awarded her their Gold Medal of Honor. In Mary's later years, as her eyes failed, she advised American collectors on which impressionist art to purchase.

1. With a partner role-play the scene between Mary Cassatt and her father in which Mary tells him why she would like to be a professional painter.
2. Can being stubborn be good and bad? Explain.
3. "Beauty is in the eye of the beholder." In the light of this statement, what do you think Mary saw in the plain girls who modeled for her?
4. From a collection of Mary's art, compare her *Bacchante* (1872) with *A Little Girl in a Blue Armchair* (1878). What differences do you notice in her style of painting? Which of the two do you like better?

SOCIAL STUDIES

1. In a reference book, read about the Louvre in Paris. What are the names of some of the great paintings that are displayed there? Choose one and find a picture of it in an art book to show to the class.
2. Look in some art books for the work of Impressionist painters. How would you describe the paintings? How do you think they compare with the kinds of paintings you enjoy?
3. What does *experimental art* mean to you? How were the Impressionists experimental? Have you ever experimented in art? How? Why?

FURTHER READING

Brooks, Philip. *Mary Cassatt: An American in Paris*. New York: Franklin Watts, 1995.

Meyer, Susan E. *Mary Cassatt*. First Impressions Series. New York: Harry N. Abrams, Inc., 1990.

Turner, Robyn Montana. *Mary Cassatt*. Portraits of Women Artists Series. Boston: Little, Brown and Company, 1994.

Venezia, Mike. *Mary Cassatt*. Getting to Know the World's Greatest Artists Series. Chicago: Childrens Press, 1990.

CÉSAR CHÁVEZ ★ 1927–1993

Agricultural Labor Union Organizer

"There's not many peppers, César. I gave you a quarter. You should have been given more. Go back to the clerk and tell him." César listened to his mother and walked back to the grocery store. The clerk was not happy about giving him more peppers. The next day the clerk, who was much bigger than César, beat him up. César remembered that his mother said he should not fight but "turn the other cheek."

César was born not long before the Great Depression (1929–1939) near Yuma, Arizona. He lived on a farm, and his father had a store. Life soon became very difficult. A drought dried up the crops, and the country around them became barren and dusty. During the Depression the banks closed and many people had no work. César's father lost his store because his customers could not pay their bills; when César's sister was born, his father paid the doctor bill with watermelons.

When told there were jobs in California picking fruits and vegetables and digging weeds, the family decided to move. Still, they had little on which to live. Sometimes César did not have socks to match. When he was teased, he said it was the new style. Then some of the other children wore unmatched socks, too.

In 1942, César was ready to graduate from the eighth grade. He had attended thirty-seven different schools because the family had had to move so much to find work.

In 1944 he joined the United States Navy. One day when he was on leave in California, he went to a movie in his uniform. A sign in the theater said Mexicans and Filipinos were to sit in a section reserved for them. Because he was a United States citizen and serving his country, he sat in the "Whites Only" section. He was immediately sent to jail. However, the police did not know what to do with him because his only offense was to sit quietly and watch a movie. They let him go, but César had learned a hard lesson about discrimination.

Throughout the 1970s and 1980s, César continued to organize farm workers so that they would get decent wages and working conditions. Six-year-old children were still found working eight to ten hours in the fields in the 1970s. In the 1980s pesticides on grapes were not only bad for consumers but were even more dangerous to the farm workers in the fields.

To call attention to the plight of the farm workers, César went on hunger strikes for many days. At other times, he and the workers marched through towns and held large rallies. The publicity brought attention to the causes for which he worked.

When César called his union to strike against the lettuce growers, he found himself in jail. But even while behind bars, he organized the prisoners to schedule their time with him in meditation, reading, exercising, and cleaning.

When he was sixty-six years old, César went on a seven-day fast to draw attention again to his beloved farm workers. They remember him as a man committed to nonviolent tactics to obtain better working conditions for agricultural workers.

1. What would you do or say if a clerk did not give you full value for a purchase you made at a grocery store? What do you think about what César Chávez did?

2. How did you feel when you read about the discrimination César experienced? Is discrimination a problem in your community? in the United States? Discuss this as a class. Give examples, if you can.

3. Write a poem or a news article about the life of César Chávez. Share it with the class.

4. Write a note to a classmate telling what you most admired about César Chávez. Ask him or her to write back what he or she most admired.

SOCIAL STUDIES

1. What is your opinion of nonviolence as an approach to solving social problems?

2. Ask a union representative to come to your class and discuss the purposes of a union. Prepare a set of questions for your class to ask him or her.

3. Talk to older people, perhaps your grandparents, who lived during the Depression. Ask them about their memories of that time. Share the things they tell you with your class.

4. Why are pesticides dangerous if left on vegetables? What can you do with store-bought raw vegetables to make them less dangerous to eat? Ask a produce manager where his or her fruits and vegetables come from.

FURTHER READING

Gonzales, Doreen. *Cesar Chavez: Leader for Migrant Farm Workers*. Hispanic Biographies Series. Springfield, NJ: Enslow Publishers, 1996.

Holmes, Burnham. *Cesar Chavez: Farm Worker Activist*. American Troublemakers Series. Austin, Texas: Raintree Steck-Vaughn Publishers, 1992.

Hoyt-Goldsmith, Diane (photographs by Lawrence Migdale). *Migrant Worker: A Boy from the Rio Grande Valley*. New York: Holiday House, 1996.

Sinnott, Susan. *Extraordinary Hispanic Americans*. Chicago, Childrens Press, 1991.

CHIANG KAI-SHEK ★ 1887–1975

Political and Military Leader

Chiang was a mischievous child. He was only three when he tried to find out how far a pair of chopsticks would go down his throat. His frightened grandfather wanted to know if he had damaged his voice box. Chiang jumped off his bed crying, "Grandson can speak, grandson not dumb."

When a tutor introduced him to Sun Tze's *The Art of War,* Chiang knew immediately that he wanted to be a soldier. Chiang went to Japan for four years for his military education. While in Japan, he joined Sun Yat-sen, a physician and Chinese revolutionary, who planned to overthrow the warlords in China. Chiang became a military officer in Sun Yat-Sen's organization.

Sun sent Chiang to the Soviet Union for further training. While there, Chiang became distrustful of the Communist party and its plans to take over his beloved China. He returned home in 1924 and trained officers who were dedicated to the cause of Sun Yat-Sen. When Sun Yat-Sen died the next year, Chiang became commander-in-chief of the National Revolutionary Army, and in a short time he was victorious over the warlord armies. By 1927 he had captured Nanking and Shanghai.

Chiang continued his attempts to unify the whole of China. His task became difficult in the late 1920s and early 1930s. Japan invaded Manchuria (northeastern China) in 1931 and then in 1937 attacked China itself. The Communists also rose up in rebellion within China, so he had two enemies with which to contend.

One good thing happened during that period. Chiang, then forty-one, met and married twenty-five-year-old Mei-ling Soong. Mei-ling was born in Shanghai but graduated from Wellesley College in Massachusetts in the United States. She helped Chiang in his efforts to bring China into modern times. Chiang also converted to Christianity, his new wife's religion.

When Japan conquered the coastal regions of China, Chiang took his government inland to a new capital, Chungking. In 1941 the United States entered World War II after Japan attacked Pearl Harbor in the Hawaiian Islands. China, at war for four years with Japan, continued its struggle for four more. Chiang knew that as soon as the war with Japan was over, he would have to fight the Communists.

Chiang's Chinese Nationalists received aid from the United States. The Soviet Union supplied the Chinese Communists. The Communists were too strong for Chiang's government, so he took his Nationalist Chinese government across the Taiwan Strait to the island of Formosa (now Taiwan).

Chiang's love for China put him in the position of fighting Chinese warlords, Communist rule, and Japanese aggression. At the end of World War II, China was recognized as one of the Big Four Allied Powers and was a founding member of the United Nations, thanks in large part to Chiang. Chiang was elected president for several terms in Taiwan and died in office at the age of eighty-seven.

1. As a small child were you ever as mischievous as Chiang? Share an incident with others and tell about the consequences.
2. How did Chiang's early mischievousness possibly help him as a leader?
3. With a small group of classmates, describe what you know about Chiang Kai-shek. The first person might say, "Chiang Kai-shek lived in. . . ." The next might give another factual statement, and so on, around the group. See how far the group can go before running out of facts.
4. List five things you would like to know more about—either about Chiang or China during his time.

SOCIAL STUDIES

1a. Find these cities on a map of China: Shanghai, Nanking (also spelled Nanjing or Nanching), and Chungking (or Chongqing or Ch'ung-ch'ing).
 b. Find these areas on a map: Japan, Manchuria (northeastern China), Formosa (Taiwan), and the Hawaiian Islands.
 c. What fourteen major countries now border China? (Find them in a clockwise direction, beginning at the Gulf of Tonkin.)
 d. Find the Taiwan Strait on a map. Approximately how far from mainland China is Taiwan?

2. In a reference book, read about the Manchu and Ch'ing dynasties in China. Share four interesting facts with the class.
3. Read about present-day China in a reference book. What impresses you most about the country?

FURTHER READING

Dolan, Sean. *Chiang Kai-Shek*. World Leaders Past & Present Series. New York: Chelsea House Publishers, 1989.

Ferroa, Peggy. *China*. Cultures of the World Series. New York: Marshall Cavendish, 1991.

JACQUES COUSTEAU ★ 1910–1997

Oceanographer

Daniel and Elizabeth Cousteau were crushed; their six-year-old boy, Jacques, was very sick. The French doctors told them he should be very quiet. But the man for whom Daniel Cousteau worked, a wealthy American, had a different idea. He encouraged the Cousteaus to teach Jacques to swim and to exercise. They listened to him, and soon Jacques was strong and healthy.

Jacques decided to become a French naval pilot. But just before he began training, he was in a car accident. Both arms were broken badly. In fact, the doctor said one should be amputated, but Jacques would not hear of this. He exercised his arm and began swimming again to gain strength. It remained bent, which kept him from flying, but otherwise he had satisfactory use of his arm.

A friend loaned Jacques a pair of swimmer's goggles. For the first time, as he swam under the water, he became aware of the beauty beneath the surface of the sea. This experience changed his life. When he told a new friend, Simone Melchoir, of this experience, she could understand. Her father, grandfather, and great-grandfather had been French admirals. Simone loved the sea, too. They married and later had two sons, Jean-Michael and Philippe.

Jacques wanted to explore within the sea for longer periods than his breath would allow. In 1943 he and others developed the Aqua-Lung, a device that enabled divers to breathe underwater for long periods of time. Now he could move freely beneath the surface with his motion-picture camera and bring undersea life to film. The device became known as a self-contained underwater breathing apparatus, or scuba, for short. The Navy used the Aqua-Lung so that divers could remove mines from the water before they could explode and sink ships.

During the 1950s Jacques bought a minesweeper that had been used to clear mines from harbors. He renamed the ship *Calypso* after a sea maiden in a Greek myth. He transformed it into a research vessel and commenced roaming the world in order to study the ocean's ecosystem.

By 1953 Jacques had written a book titled *The Silent World*. It was translated into twenty-two languages and sold over five million copies. Then he created a full-length film by the same name.

On one trip, when the *Calypso* was between Madagascar and the Seychelles island of Aldabra, the winds were high and the crew sought refuge in an island harbor to wait for the storm to end. The harbor's waters were calm and the scene below the water was strikingly beautiful. Delightful fish gathered all around them when the divers entered the water. One fish became their friend. It was a sixty-pound grouper that they named Ulysses.

Over the years, Jacques made many movies and television productions about undersea life. He helped stop the dumping of nuclear waste in the sea and made people more aware of the harmful effects of ocean pollution. Most of all, Jacques brought the beauty and magic of the undersea world to life for millions of people.

1. Write a sentence with exactly fourteen words telling something about Jacques Cousteau. Exchange sentences with a partner and compare them. Return the paper with a sentence of exactly ten words telling something else you know about Jacques.

2. Draw a cartoon showing Jacques—wearing goggles for the first time—meeting an underwater fish. Give the fish a name. What do they say to each other?

3. What more would you like to know about exploring the ocean? List three things. See if you can find the answers in reference books.

SOCIAL STUDIES

1. The continents divide the ocean, which covers seventy percent of the Earth's surface, into three major oceans. What are they, in order from greatest to smallest size? A smaller, fourth ocean lies north of Asia, Europe, and North America. Which one is it? Which ocean is nearest you?

2. Which ocean do you think would be the most interesting to explore? Why?

3. Locate Madagascar and the Seychelles island of Aldabra on a map or globe. In what ocean are they found? Read about these two places in a reference book and share two interesting facts with the class.

4. At the library or video store, find a video made by Jacques Cousteau. Watch it at home and prepare to tell the class about it.

FURTHER READING

Greene, Carol. *Jacques Cousteau: Man of the Oceans*. Rookie Biography Series. Chicago, IL: Childrens Press, 1990.

Reef, Catherine. *Jacques Cousteau: Champion of the Sea*. Earthkeepers Series. Frederick, MD: Twenty-First Century Books, 1992.

CRAZY HORSE ★ 1844?–1877

Oglala Sioux Indian Chief

He was nicknamed "Curly," although his hair was long and straight. His complexion was light, not like that of the other Sioux Indians with whom he lived. On this day, as a thirteen-year-old, he sat in the hills with the old men of the tribe and watched the young warriors discuss a cow with United States government soldiers. The cow had run off from its Mormon owner and stormed through the Sioux camp. The animal was killed by a member of the tribe. The people promptly ate it.

Chief Conquering Bear offered a fine pony as retribution. But the United States Army officer Lieutenant John L. Grattan refused the offer. He wanted the Sioux Indian who killed the cow. The Sioux warrior would not give himself up. The lieutenant ordered his men to fire, and Conquering Bear, with nine bullets in his body, fell dead. Immediately, Sioux warriors came out of hiding and killed the thirty-one soldiers.

Curly was overwhelmed by the sight and went off to seek a vision from the spirit for his role as a Sioux. After three days of fasting and meditating, Curly received his vision. His father, also named Crazy Horse, interpreted the vision and gave Curly the name Crazy Horse. His father then took the name Worm.

According to his vision, he was to wear a single hawk feather, paint a streak of lightning across his face prior to a battle, take no scalps, and care for and lead his people rather than think of himself.

Crazy Horse was not always true to his vision. He killed two Arapaho Indians and took their scalps. In that same battle he received an arrow wound in his leg. The wound was his reminder that he should not take scalps.

The land of the Powder River country was given to the Sioux in a treaty with the United States government for "as long as buffalo may range thereon in such numbers as to justify the chase." How long the buffalo would be there was unknown, too, because many white "sportsmen" came and killed the buffalo for sport and not for food.

In 1862 gold was found in Montana. The route to Montana, called the Bozeman Trail, went right through the Powder River Territory, which was Sioux land. War with the white men was inevitable.

The Civil War was over in 1865. By 1874 many white men began streaming across the country, seeking gold and land. The Sioux, led by Crazy Horse, fought fiercely and won several battles against the United States Army.

Finally, Crazy Horse saw that there were too many "bluecoats." His people could not possibly defeat all the white soldiers and keep their own land. Crazy Horse was given many promises by the United States government, but these promises were not kept. Crazy Horse surrendered, and the army put him in jail. In his attempt to escape, he was struck through the back with a bayonet and died a few hours later. The Sioux people mourned for Crazy Horse because they knew he always loved them and cared for them.

1. What instances of injustice to Crazy Horse and his tribe did you read about in this biography? Discuss these situations.
2. Compose three newspaper headlines about Crazy Horse at different periods in his life.
3. Were any parts of the life of Crazy Horse confusing to you? If so, discuss them with your teacher and classmates.
4. If you could change the ending of this biography, how would you do it?

SOCIAL STUDIES

1. Read about the Sioux Indians in a reference book. Share three interesting facts with the class.
2. Who were the "bluecoats"?
3. In reference books, or from the reading list that follows, find map illustrations of the Bozeman Trail and the Powder River Territory. What states do these areas now include?

FURTHER READING

Guttmacher, Peter. *Crazy Horse: Sioux War Chief*. North American Indians of Achievement Series. New York: Chelsea House Publishers, 1994.

St. George, Judith. *Crazy Horse*. New York: Putnam Publishing Group, 1994.

Sanford, William R. *Crazy Horse: Sioux Warrior*. North American Leaders of the Wild West Series. Springfield, NJ: Enslow Publishers, 1994.

MARIE CURIE

★ 1867?–1934

Scientist

The little Polish girl, Manya (*Marie* in French), was only four. Her sister, Bronya, was seven and learning to read. To pass the time together, Bronya cut letters of the alphabet from cardboard and leaned them against the wall. Together, they played school. But when Bronya had difficulty reading her lesson for their parents, Manya took the book and read it perfectly. The parents were stunned. Their youngest child had learned to read on her own!

Manya continued to amaze everyone. As she grew older, she concentrated so hard on the books she read that she was not aware of what was going on around her. Sometimes her three sisters and brother would build a pyramid of chairs around her. When she got up from reading, the chairs would tumble down around her. "That's stupid!" she would say and stalk out of the room.

As Manya grew older, she attended an illegal night school in Warsaw called the "floating university." The classes met at different locations four nights a week, often in basements and living rooms, all to evade the Russians. Still, Manya wanted to get an education some place where she could do experiments and become a real scientist.

Then Manya had an idea. She took a job as a governess for a few years so that Bronya could go to Paris to study for her medical degree. Manya sent money from her pay each month. When Bronya graduated, she got a job and helped Manya through school.

Finally, in 1891, Manya enrolled in the Sorbonne in Paris as Marie Sklodowska. Marie lived in a tiny attic close to the Sorbonne. She studied so hard that she often forgot to eat. Her room was very cold and she became ill. When her sister found out, she insisted that Marie come live with her and her husband.

Two years later, Marie received the first physics degree granted to a woman at the Sorbonne. The next year, she earned a degree in mathematics. She now could return to Warsaw and get a job as a teacher to help her country.

But a tall, handsome French scientist named Pierre Curie appeared in her life. They had much in common. They talked about science and what they wanted to accomplish in life. In 1895 they were married and later had two children. Now Marie was a teacher, a scientist, a wife, and a mother. She decided to get a doctorate in physics!

Marie and Pierre worked together and discovered two new elements (matter made up of one type of atom), which they named polonium and radium. They received the Nobel Prize for physics in 1903, and Marie received a second Nobel Prize in 1911 for chemistry.

Pierre was killed in an accident in 1906, and Marie took over his professorship. She was the first woman to teach at the Sorbonne in Paris.

She died in 1934 of pernicious anemia caused by radium poisoning. The same rays that would save many lives in the future took Marie Curie to her death.

1. What one thing impressed you most about Marie Curie? Compare your answer with a partner's.
2. Make a list of some of the things Marie accomplished. Then make a list of several things you would like to accomplish in your life. What steps can you take to prepare to achieve these goals?
3. Pretend you are walking down a street in Paris and Marie Curie walks along beside you. She invites you to have tea with her at a little cafe. What will you talk about? What might you ask her? Write a list of questions.

4. What were the most difficult words in the biography to understand? Study these words together in a small group.

SOCIAL STUDIES

1. On a globe, place your finger on the spot where you are now. Trace your finger to Warsaw, Poland, and then Paris, France. In what direction are you from those two places?
2. Read about the element radium in a reference book. What are some of its uses? Why is it dangerous?
3. What is the Nobel Prize? Look it up in a reference book with a partner. How many Nobel Prizes are awarded each year? In what areas? Can you think of other achievements that should be honored by a Nobel Prize?

FURTHER READING

Brandt, Keith. Marie Curie: *Brave Scientist*. Mahwah, NJ: Troll Communications, 1983.

Grady, Sean M. *Marie Curie*. San Diego, CA: Lucent Books, Inc., 1992.

Poynter, Margaret. *Marie Curie: Discoverer of Radium*. Great Minds of Science Series. Hillside, NJ: Enslow Publishers, Inc., 1994.

Steinke, Ann E. *Marie Curie and the Discovery of Radium*. Hauppauge, NY: Barron's Educational Series, Inc., 1987.

Stille, Darlene R. *Extraordinary Women Scientists*. Chicago, IL: Childrens Press, 1995.

JOSEPH DAMIEN DE VEUSTER ★ 1840–1889

Priest and Missionary

There were two books in young Joseph's farm home in Belgium: the Bible and a two-foot-high volume of *The Lives of the Saints*. His mother, Catherine, often read from both of these. Joseph was intrigued with the stories of martyrs and hermits in the book about saints. He enjoyed staying quiet and pretending to be a hermit.

One day when he was eight years old, he convinced four of his brothers and sisters to skip school and spend the day hidden in the fields as hermits. That whole day they said nothing. A search party of Joseph's worried parents and friends found them later in the afternoon.

Formal schooling ended when Joseph was thirteen. He worked on the farm and became very strong.

But Joseph was drawn to the parish church, not farming. His father reluctantly agreed to his choosing the priesthood, and Joseph joined a small Catholic missionary order with his older brother, Auguste, in nearby Louvain. Joseph took the name *Damien* from a fourth-century physician who, without charge, treated people who were ill. Damien's brother took the name *Pamphile*.

Pamphile was chosen to be a missionary in the Sandwich Islands (now the Hawaiian Islands), but he came down with typhus. Damien nursed him back to health. However, Pamphile was still too weak to become a missionary, so Damien wrote to his superiors in Paris and asked to be allowed to take his brother's place.

In November 1863 he left Bremerhaven, Germany. By December, he was crossing the equator on the sailing ship *R. W. Wood*. They rounded Cape Horn, went through a terrible storm, and reached the islands in March.

Damien enjoyed his work as a priest. He used his strength and farm skills to build a number of churches in Hawaii. Yet he was worried about the natives, for many were ill and died from infectious diseases brought to the island by foreign sailors. One of the worst diseases was leprosy. Leprosy produced large open sores, swelling, tumors, and destruction of the mucous membranes in the respiratory tract and eyes. The tip of one island, Molokai, was set aside for people with the disease.

For sixteen years Damien comforted the people on Molokai. He built a church and school with his own hands and learned to do operations from a doctor there who had the disease.

While Father Damien was living on Molokai, a Norwegian physician named Gerhard Hansen found that leprosy is caused by bacteria. His discovery had led to improved treatment of the "death before death," as it has been called. Modern drugs are now used to control the disease, which is known as Hansen's disease.

The day came when Father Damien realized that he, too, had Hansen's disease. Because of his compassion and work, many people around the world learned of Damien and Hansen's disease. Others came to help him. One was an artist who did a charcoal drawing of Damien. When asked to sign it, Damien wrote, "I was sick and ye visited me. J. Damien de Veuster."

1. Write a letter to Father Damien telling him how you feel about his sacrificing himself for the lepers on Molokai.
2. Joseph took the name Damien from a fourth-century physician. If you could add another name to your present one, what would you choose? Why?
3. Fold a blank sheet of paper in half the long way. In the left column, write key words or phrases from the biography that describe Damien or what he did. In the right column, write a thought you have in reaction to each word or phrase you listed. For example, on the left you might write, "pretending to be a hermit." On the right, you might write, "No wonder he became a priest."
4. Why would Damien write on his charcoal portrait, "I was sick and ye visited me"?
5. What does the phrase "the death before death" mean?

SOCIAL STUDIES

1. With your finger, trace on a map or globe the route Damien took from Bremerhaven, Germany, around Cape Horn of South America to the Hawaiian Islands. What countries did he pass on his left and right?
2. Find the Hawaiian Islands on a map or globe. From where you are at this moment, in what direction would you go to get there?
3. What profession do you think is most important to humanity? Why?

FURTHER READING

Brown, Pam. *Father Damien: The Man Who Lived and Died for the Victims of Leprosy*. People Who Have Helped the World Series. Milwaukee, WI: Gareth Stevens Publishing, 1987.

McNair, Sylvia. *Hawaii*. America the Beautiful Series. Chicago: Childrens Press, 1989.

BILLIE DAVIS ★ 1923–

Educator, Missionary, Writer

In a beat-up old truck or car, Billie and her family traveled throughout the West. During the 1920s and 1930s, they followed the crops as they became ripe for harvesting. Farmers needed help during the planting and harvesting seasons, but when there were no crops for harvesting, the family was out of work. They were called migratory workers, farm laborers, transients, Oakies, and migrants.

Billie's family, made up of her parents and eight children, was constantly on the road looking for work. When they stopped for the night, they pitched a tent. The family worked in every state west of the Mississippi.

Billie found churches, libraries, and schools along the way. In a schoolyard playground, she and her sister would play on the swings and pretend they were at their very own school. At age seven, in a Sunday school class, she sat in a real chair for the first time.

Billie was eight when the family stayed in one place long enough for her to go to school for a few weeks. Billie started in close to forty schools that she had to leave when the family moved on. Public schools, libraries, and Sunday schools were her places of refuge, for she loved to learn. In her senior year, the family lived in one place for a full year. That year, Billie took courses in history, drama, English, and Spanish. In the evenings, she went "home" and ate by a campfire. She did her homework by the light of a kerosene lamp. Nevertheless, despite these hard conditions, Billie was the editor of the school newspaper and yearbook and she was on the varsity debate team.

Eventually, Billie was able to use her meager savings to go to Drury College in Springfield, Missouri, where she majored in sociology and Spanish. She graduated at the top of her class. Graduate work in sociology at the University of Missouri followed. While there, she met and married a young man named George H. Davis, who was attending Central Bible College.

Billie wrote of her experiences as a "hobo" kid for the *Saturday Evening Post*. People who read it were captivated. She spoke to thousands of teachers around the country.

From Missouri, Billie and George went to Latin America as missionaries for the Assemblies of God churches. While in Costa Rica, they adopted a poor and undernourished seven-year-old child named Gloria who weighed only twenty-nine pounds. When they returned to the United States, Gloria went to public school and then college and afterward became a speech therapist.

Billie taught migrant youth in a special program at the University of Miami. She also attended classes there and received a master's degree and then her doctorate in education.

George and Billie went to Belgium as missionaries and later lived in Springfield, Missouri, where Billie became a professor and department chairperson at Evangel College. She still conducts educational and religious seminars around the country.

1. Write three or four sentences telling why you think Billie Davis is inspiring.
2. In your imagination, think of what it would be like to live in a tent most of your early life. What do you think you would miss the most? For five minutes, write your thoughts as fast as you can. Share them with a partner who has done this same exercise.
3. Copy two sentences from the biography that you think are factual and two that you think are opinion. Discuss with a classmate your reasons for the choices you made.

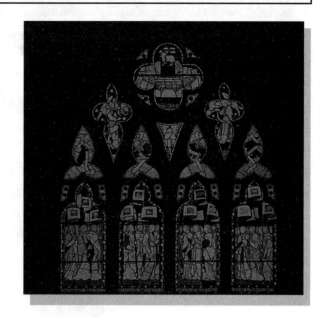

SOCIAL STUDIES

1. On a map, count the number of mainland states west of the Mississippi where Billie and her family worked in the fields. How many are there? Which is your favorite?
2. Billie lived in Springfield, Missouri (Drury College); St. Louis, Missouri (University of Missouri); Miami, Florida (University of Miami); Costa Rica; and Belgium. After you have found these places on a map or globe, rank them in order, from the one you would most like to visit to the one you would least like to visit. Compare your rankings with your classmates'.

3. Read more about migrant workers in a reference book. See if you can write a short story about a migrant child.
4. When you go out to your school's playground, pretend with a friend that you are migrant children. Take notes on what you say to each other. Discuss your conversation with the class.

FURTHER READING

Gates, Doris. *Blue Willow*. New York: Viking Children's Books, 1940; Puffin Books, 1976.

Altman, Linda J. *Amelia's Road*. New York: Lee Low Books, 1993.

Hoyt-Goldsmith, Diane (photographs by Lawrence Migdale). *Migrant Worker: A Boy From the Rio Grande Valley*. New York: Holiday House, 1996.

Williams, Shirley Anne. *Working Cotton*. New York: Harcourt Brace Children's Books, 1992.

WALT DISNEY ★ 1901–1966

Motion Picture Cartoonist and Producer

Walt memorized Abraham Lincoln's Gettysburg Address in the fifth grade. One day when he went to school, he carried his father's coat, a cardboard top hat blackened with shoe polish, and a homemade beard. On his cheek he put some putty to resemble the wart on Lincoln's chin. His Gettysburg Address was so delightful that the teacher invited the principal to hear it. The principal then took Walt to all the other classes in the school to give the speech.

Years later, Walt Disney developed Audio-Animatronics—special robot-like copies of United States presidents, so lifelike they appear real. The robot, Abraham Lincoln, has fifteen facial movements and forty-eight different body actions. His animated Abraham Lincoln has shaped the way millions of people think of famous presidents.

Walt's early life was controlled by his father, Elias, who did not believe in giving "useless" Christmas and birthday gifts. Useful gifts were socks or underwear.

After serving as a Red Cross ambulance driver in World War I, Walt returned to Kansas City and made sketches for an advertising company. He learned to do animations of his cartoons by photographing a series of drawings. The shape of each drawing would change a little bit, so that when the photographs were flipped quickly, it looked as if the drawings were moving.

During the 1920s and early 1930s, animated cartoons filled the time between full-length features at movie theaters. Most animated movie cartoons were only six minutes long, although some cartoon features ran for twenty minutes. From such cartoons, Walt Disney and his cartoon characters, such as Mickey Mouse, Donald Duck, and Pluto, became known worldwide.

Walt decided to make a ninety-minute, full-length cartoon. People in the movie business called it "Disney's Folly" and said no one would sit that long for a cartoon. But Walt made *Snow White and the Seven Dwarfs*, and it became the most popular cartoon film ever made. This was followed by cartoon films such as *Fantasia*, *Bambi*, and *101 Dalmatians*.

Walt and Lillian, his wife, had a child, Diane, and then adopted baby Sharon. The little girls were not aware that their father was well known. One day, Diane came home from school after learning from her friends how important he was. She asked her father, "Are you Walt Disney?" When he answered, "Yes," she asked him for his autograph.

Walt often took his daughters to amusement parks on weekends and he waited for them on park benches while they rode the various rides. It disturbed him to see paper blowing around on the grounds and the poor-quality food that was sold. He thought that some day he would make a much better park, and he did. Disneyland was created in Anaheim, California, and the even bigger Walt Disney World was opened in Orlando, Florida. Now families go to Walt's parks, where the grounds are neat and clean, the food is good, and adults as well as kids enjoy themselves.

1. Choose an incident in Walt Disney's or his children's lives (from the biography or your imagination) and draw a filmstrip with several pictures illustrating that incident.

2. Using three to five words, write five titles about Walt Disney. "Walt Disney:

_____

_____

_____

_____

_____

3. What is your favorite Disney cartoon or movie? Write a short summary of it and exchange your summary with one written by a classmate. Write a positive comment at the end of your classmate's summary.

4. Pretend you are sitting on a park bench with Walt as he watches his daughters on amusement park rides. Tell him what he is going to create in the future. Is he surprised?

SOCIAL STUDIES

1. Pretend Walt Disney has asked you and a small group of classmates for advice about planning a new theme park in your state or community. What does your group tell him? Where would you recommend putting it? Why? Would there be adequate highways for the traffic? What theme should the park have? What rides? Take notes on your group's recommendations.

2. Learn more about cartoon animation in reference books. Share two interesting facts with the class.

FURTHER READING

Barrett, Katherine and Richard. *The Man Behind the Magic: The Story of Walt Disney*. New York: Viking Children's Books, 1991.

DOROTHEA LYNDE DIX ★ 1802–1887

Advocate for the Mentally Ill

Dorothea loved visiting her grandfather and grandmother. Grandfather Dix had a large library and taught Dorothea to read. She did not want to go home, for at home she had to care for her two younger brothers and her mother, who was frequently ill. Her father was often away, traveling by horseback and preaching in small churches around the countryside. Dorothea taught her brothers to read, just as her grandfather had taught her.

When she turned twelve, Dorothea ran away from home to her grandmother's in Boston. She persuaded her grandmother to keep her. Two years later, she was sent to live with an aunt in Worcester, Massachusetts. There, at age fourteen, Dorothea opened a school of her own and taught for three years.

During the next thirty years, Dorothea attended school, studied with private tutors, opened an academy for wealthy young women in her grandmother's home, and operated a free school for children of the poor.

But in 1851, illness forced Dorothea to stop teaching. She spent two years recovering in Europe. Then she volunteered to teach a Sunday School class for young women in jail. At that time, mentally ill people were sent to jail because there was no other place for them. It was cold and damp in the cells. The young women pleaded for heat. The jailer told Dorothea, "Don't worry about them. Insane people don't feel the cold."

Dorothea Dix now knew her mission in life. She traveled throughout the state of Massachusetts visiting jails, workhouses, and hospitals. She filled notebooks with information on the conditions she found.

Dorothea wrote a report that was made available to the public. Many people became angry at hearing of the abuse suffered by the mentally ill. Others could not believe such things could happen. In her report, she told about mentally ill people being locked in cages, closets, cellars, and pens. They were chained, stripped of their clothing, beaten with rods, and lashed for disobedience.

Dorothea visited throughout the Northeast, Midwest, and the South. She found the same cruel conditions everywhere she went. Generous people who had a great deal of money—philanthropists—gave of their wealth, and state legislatures appropriated money. Soon, new hospitals were built for the mentally ill.

Dorothea was fifty-nine years old when the Civil War began, and she volunteered. Because of her work around hospitals, she was appointed superintendent of nurses. One of the women who came to Dorothea for nurses' training was Louisa May Alcott, who later wrote *Little Women*. Louisa also wrote *Hospital Sketches*, which told about her experiences as a nurse during the Civil War.

Dorothea continued to work after the war. She retired when she was eighty years old. Her last years were spent at Trenton State Hospital, where she lived in a fine apartment and entertained her many friends.

1. Write a brief obituary for Dorothea Dix. Be sure to include her most notable achievements.

2. Dorothea learned that her mission in life was to help the mentally ill. Make a list of four or five things you would like to do for others in your lifetime. Make a copy and ask a trusted family member to save it for you in a safe place until you are older.

3. Why do you think the jailers thought mentally ill people felt no pain in the cold? Write your answer in a short paragraph.

4. What is a philanthropist? What would you have to do to become one? If you became one, what charities would you enjoy helping?

SOCIAL STUDIES

1. The mentally ill used to be called *insane*. Why is *mentally ill* a better term? Write in thirty words or less what the term *mentally ill* means to you. Share your answer with a small group.

2. Read parts of Louisa May Alcott's *Hospital Sketches* and report the most interesting part to your class.

3. Invite a mental health counselor from your local hospital or mental health facility to come to your class. As a class, prepare a set of questions to ask him or her about mental health problems, how the mentally ill are treated, and what you can do to help.

FURTHER READING

Malone, Mary. *Dorothea L. Dix: Hospital Founder*. Discovery Biography Series. New York: Chelsea Juniors, 1991.

FREDERICK DOUGLASS ★ 1817–1895

Orator, Journalist, Antislavery Leader

Little Frederick's mother, Harriet, was a slave on a plantation. After Frederick was born, she was given only a week to rest; then she had to go back to the fields to work from sunrise to sunset. Frederick's Grandmama Betsy took care of him on another plantation twelve miles away. Harriet sometimes walked the twelve miles after dark to see her little boy. But she had to walk back the same night so she could begin work the next day.

When Frederick was six, he was old enough to work as a slave. His Grandmama dropped him off at another plantation, where he fed the chickens and cleaned up around the farm.

When he turned eight years old, the wife of Frederick's slave master made Frederick a companion to her little boy. Frederick enjoyed this job and learned to read along with his young white friend.

Frederick practiced reading every chance he got. He found old newspapers in trash cans and read them. One day, he found the word *abolitionist* in a newspaper and learned that it referred to a person who wanted to abolish, or stop, slavery. He was surprised to find out that some white people were against slavery.

When he was twenty-two years old, Frederick was able to run away from his master and head north. He escaped from the South with the help of Anna Murray, a freed slave whom he married. He also changed his name from Frederick Augustus Washington Bailey to Frederick Douglass. He had a wife, a new name, and a new life, but still he was not free.

In the North he met white people who helped him. Since he was still legally a slave, he could be kidnapped and sent back to his master at any time. There were people whose job was to find runaway slaves and return them to their owners.

Frederick discovered that he could express himself well in front of an audience. He told people of the evils of slavery.

In 1845 Frederick wrote his autobiography, *Narrative of the Life of Frederick Douglass*. This made him well known, and his friends feared he would be taken back to his slave master. So Frederick went to Europe, where he gave antislavery speeches and raised money for the movement to abolish slavery in America. While he was there, friends collected money and sent it to his owner to buy his freedom. At last Frederick was free.

He came back to the United States and began a newspaper called *The North Star* to speak out against slavery. The name referred to the star in the night sky that he and other slaves followed as they escaped to the North.

The Civil War began in 1861, and Frederick advocated using black men in the army. His sons joined the Union Army. Even though black soldiers were enlisted, they received only half the pay of white soldiers.

With the war over, Frederick spoke out for equal rights for women and their right to vote. In his later years, he became president of the Freedman's Savings and Trust Company, a United States marshal, and the U.S. consul general to Haiti.

64

People of Purpose

1. What sentence in the biography of Frederick Douglass outraged you the most? Why? What sentence inspired you the most?

2. At six years of age, Frederick began working as a slave on a farm. At six years of age, what could you do on a farm? List five things.

3. Write a letter to a relative telling about Frederick Douglass. Share with a partner what you wrote.

4. Frederick practiced reading anything he could find. If you had no books or newspapers, what could you find around your house or neighborhood to read? List five things.

SOCIAL STUDIES

1. Why did slave owners not want slaves to learn how to read? What do you think they were afraid of? Write a paragraph telling three to five things reading can do for a person.

2. Pretend you are an abolitionist. Write a short speech against slavery. Give your speech to the class.

3. Why do you think black Union soldiers received only half the pay of white Union soldiers?

4. If Frederick could come back today, what would he think about the movement toward equality of the sexes and races?

FURTHER READING

Altman, Susan. *Extraordinary Black Americans from Colonial to Contemporary Times*. Chicago: Childrens Press, 1989.

Bennett, Evelyn. *Frederick Douglass and the War Against Slavery*. Gateway Civil Rights Series. Brookfield, CT: The Millbrook Press, 1993.

Douglass, Frederick. *Escape from Slavery: The Boyhood of Frederick Douglass in His Own Words*. New York: Knopf Books for Young Readers, 1994.

Kerby, Mona. *Frederick Douglass*. New York: Franklin Watts, 1994.

Lester, Julius. *To Be a Slave*. New York: Scholastic, 1986.

McKissack, Patricia and Fredrick. *Frederick Douglass: Leader Against Slavery*. Great African Americans Series. Hillside, NJ: Enslow Publishers, 1991.

Patterson, Lillie. *Frederick Douglass: Freedom Fighter*. Champaign, IL: Champaign Publishing Company, 1965.

Russell, Sharman. *Frederick Douglass: Abolitionist Editor*. Black Americans of Achievement Series. New York: Chelsea House Publishers, 1988.

Santrey, Laurence. *Young Frederick Douglass: Fight for Freedom*. Mahwah, NJ: Troll Communications, 1983.

AMELIA EARHART ★ 1897–1937?

Aviator

Amelia had a great idea: Why not build a roller coaster? She was seven years old when she, her five-year-old sister, Muriel, and a neighbor boy built a track out of scrap lumber. They laid the track from the top of an old shed to the ground. Then they added roller-skate wheels to a board to carry them. Amelia went first and crashed, and then she crashed again. The children repaired the track and extended it so they could roll across the lawn. "This is just like flying!" Amelia shouted when they finally were able to roll down the tracks without crashing. But Amelia's mother made them take their roller coaster apart before they hurt themselves "flying."

Amelia went to college, but she did not find that what she learned was very practical. In 1917, when visiting her sister in Toronto, Canada, she saw Canadian soldiers who had lost arms and legs in the war. She dropped out of college and took a first-aid course given by the Red Cross. Soon she was scrubbing floors and doing the work of a nurse's aide.

In 1920 Amelia was in California at an airshow. Retired army pilots were entertaining audiences with their stunt flying. Amelia paid a flyer to give her a one-dollar, ten-minute ride over Hollywood, and she was hooked!

Amelia took flying lessons with Neta "Snooky" Snook. Snooky made her learn all about an airplane before she gave her flying lessons. Amelia became a mechanic and repaired engines. Then she learned the parts of the airplane. After that, Snooky took Amelia in the air and gave her practice in all the flying maneuvers. Amelia began to look like a pilot. She dressed like the men and cut her long hair until it was quite short.

In 1928 she was asked to be a passenger, the only female, on a flight to Great Britain. She accepted and became the first woman to fly across the Atlantic. Soon people all over the world heard about her. That same year, she flew solo back and forth across the United States—the first woman to do so. In 1932 she became the first woman to fly solo across the Atlantic.

Amelia won so many awards and set so many records that people wondered what else she could do. In the back of her mind she was thinking of one last, great flight. She wanted, in her words, "to fly around the globe at its waistline."

After some setbacks, she and her navigator, Fred Noonan, flew from Oakland, California, to Miami, Florida, then to South America, and then across the Atlantic and Africa to India. Some days later, they landed in New Guinea and headed for Howland Island, a small spot of land in the middle of the Pacific just above the equator. The island was two miles long and one-half mile wide. Amelia and Fred never arrived there. It was assumed that they ran out of fuel and the airplane went down into the Pacific Ocean. No wreckage was ever found.

Amelia changed people's ideas about the place of women in aviation and showed that women could pioneer new fields.

1. How was Amelia as a child similar to Amelia as an adult? Draw a picture of Amelia on the roller coaster or on her sled. Give the picture a title.

2. Why do you suppose Amelia wore men's clothing and cut her hair short when flying?

3. With a partner, create a poem about Amelia's last flight. Share it with your classmates.

SOCIAL STUDIES

1. What did Amelia mean by saying she wanted "to fly around the globe at its waistline"?

2. What records are still to be set by men and women in space? Discuss your list with your class.

3. With a small group, use a globe or map to trace the route of Amelia and Fred Noonan on their flight around the earth:
   —Oakland, California, U.S.A.
   —Burbank, California, U.S.A.
   —Tucson, Arizona, U.S.A.
   —New Orleans, Louisiana, U.S.A.
   —Miami, Florida, U.S.A.
   —San Juan, Puerto Rico, a commonwealth of the U.S.A.
   —Caripito, Venezuela
   —Paramaribo, Suriname
   —Fortaleza, Brazil
   —Natal, Brazil
   —Saint-Louis, Senegal
   —Dakar, Senegal
   —Gao, Mali
   —Fort-Lamy (now N'djamena), Chad
   —El Fasher, Sudan
   —Khartoum, Sudan
   —Massawa, Eritrea
   —Assab, Eritrea
   —Karachi, Pakistan
   —Calcutta, India
   —Akyab, Myanmar (formerly Burma)
   —Rangoon (now Yangon), Myanmar
   —Singapore
   —Bandoeng (now Bandung), Indonesia
   —Saurabaya (also spelled Surabaya), Indonesia
   —Koepang (now Kupang), Indonesia (on the island of Timor)
   —Port Darwin (now Darwin), Australia
   —Lae, New Guinea
   —Howland Island, U.S.A. (uninhabited) 0.48N 176.38°W (contact lost)

4. Compare the childhoods of Amelia Earhart and Charles Lindbergh.

FURTHER READING

Chadwick, Roxane. *Amelia Earhart: Aviation Pioneer*. Achievers Series. Minneapolis, MN: Lerner Group, 1987.

Parlin, John. *Amelia Earhart: Pioneer in the Sky*. Discovery Biography Series. New York: Chelsea Juniors, 1992.

Sabin, Francene. *Amelia Earhart: Adventure in the Sky*. Mahwah, NJ: Troll Communications, 1983.

Shore, Nancy. *Amelia Earhart*. American Women of Achievement Series. New York: Chelsea House Publishers, 1987.

Yount, Lisa. *Women Aviators*. American Profiles Series. New York: Facts on File, 1995.

THOMAS A. EDISON ★ 1847–1931

Inventor and Industrial Leader

Although Thomas Edison became a brilliant inventor, his early school years were difficult. His first teacher called him "addled," meaning muddled or confused in his thinking. Perhaps it was because Thomas was always asking questions. He wanted to know why chickens sat on eggs. When he did not get a straight answer from his teacher, Thomas tried sitting on some eggs the way hens do. The result: disaster!

Once, after a train stop, Thomas was late returning. He ran frantically after the train. The conductor caught Thomas by the ears and hauled him aboard. His ears hurt for sometime afterward, so he went to the doctor. The doctor said he was going to lose his hearing. Whether it was because of the train boarding episode or a previous bout with scarlet fever, no one knows for sure. But Thomas did lose a lot of his hearing as he grew older.

Thomas found work as a telegraph operator in places around the country. He decided to become a "practical" inventor. His inventions would have to be useful for people. Thomas's first patented invention was a vote-recording machine.

At twenty-four Thomas married a young woman named Mary Stilwell. They had three children. Thomas humorously nicknamed the first two children "Dot" and "Dash" after the sounds he made on the telegraph key.

An invention by Thomas Edison that we all use is the electric light bulb. Thomas tried using many different things inside the bulb to cause it to burn for long periods and produce light: platinum, carbon thread, and bamboo. Tungsten was the metal that finally became the filament that worked. To show off his invention to the world, he invited reporters and influential people to Menlo Park, New Jersey, where he and his assistants worked on inventions. He strung lights all over the area. When it was dark, he turned the switch and the people thought they were in fairyland. They cheered and cheered. Some stayed throughout the night to gaze in wonder.

Mary, his wife, suddenly died of typhoid fever. Now Thomas had both his work and the three children to care for. He met Mina Miller. He taught her Morse code, and one day he tapped a question on her arm: "Will you marry me?" She tapped back, "Yes." They also had three children.

Mina was a great help to Thomas. Because of his hearing problem, Thomas had difficulty understanding when he was in a crowd of people. Mina tapped messages on his arm so he could understand the conversations around him.

Thomas created the kinetoscope (projector) and set up a movie studio in West Orange, New Jersey, where his invention factory was relocated. He made a new grade of cement, and 180,000 bags of it helped construct Yankee Stadium in New York City. Before he died at eighty-four, Thomas obtained 1,093 patents for his inventions—many of which we use today and probably take for granted. He and other inventors of that period made the United States an industrial world power.

1. What did you find most inspiring about Thomas Edison? Make a list of ten words describing him.
2. Thomas wanted to make practical inventions. Why were his practical? Draw an example of a practical and an impractical invention. Share your examples with the class.
3. Thomas Edison once said, "Genius is one percent inspiration and ninety-nine percent perspiration." What does that statement mean to you?

SOCIAL STUDIES

1. What does it mean to patent an invention?
2. Do further study of Edison's many inventions. Make a list of some of them. Choose one and give a short report on it to the class.
3. Make up a short question and learn to tap it out in Morse code, as Thomas did to Mina. You can find the Morse code in a reference book. Practice your question on a partner.
4. With a partner, see if you can make up an invention that would be useful in some way. Draw a picture of your invention and explain to the class how it works.

FURTHER READING

Buranelli, Vincent. *Thomas Alva Edison.* Pioneers in Change Series. Englewood Cliffs, NJ: Silver Burdett Press, 1992.

Guthridge, Sue. *Thomas A. Edison: Young Inventor.* Childhood of Famous Americans Series. New York: Macmillan, 1986.

Kaufman, Mervyn D. *Thomas Alva Edison: Miracle Maker.* Discovery Biographies Series. New York: Chelsea House, 1993.

Lampton, Christopher. *Thomas Alva Edison.* Tarrytown, NY: Marshall Cavendish, 1991.

Nirgiotis, Nicholas. *Thomas Edison.* Cornerstones of Freedom Series. Chicago, IL: Childrens Press, 1994.

ALBERT EINSTEIN ★ 1879–1955

Scientist

Albert Einstein is the most famous scientist of the twentieth century. He did not work in a laboratory with test tubes and whirling gadgets. He did not even talk until he was three years old. In fact, he did not speak well until he was nine years old. Yet he asked difficult questions and used his mind as his imaginative laboratory.

When he was five years old, Albert was sick in bed. His father brought him a compass to amuse him. Then the questions began. Why does the compass needle point to the north? Something invisible must do this. What is it? In later life he would write, "Something deeply hidden had to be behind things." Even so, the principal of the school Albert attended said, "He'll never make a success of anything."

Albert studied for a college degree in Zurich, Switzerland, at the National Polytechnic Institute. A job at the Swiss Patent Office opened and he worked there for several years. In this job Albert had to write down complex ideas in simple words so that others could understand them. In the evenings and on weekends, he used his mind to think about the many questions that he had about time, light, energy, space, gravity, and motion.

In his mind he related these ideas to real-life things, such as clocks and speeding trains. By doing this, he made his difficult ideas understandable to himself and others. Even so, many people still did not understand them.

While he worked in the Patent Office, he wrote scientific papers about his thoughts and sent them off for others to read. In 1905 his *Special Theory of Relativity* was published. Albert thought that speed affects time and an object's mass and length as it nears the speed of light. He gave the world a famous mathematical equation to explain this theory: $E=mc2$.

Then he wrote on the *General Theory of Relativity*. In this theory he described the way gravity depends on curves in space and how these curves are caused by the size of stars and planets. He helped scientists understand the way gravity affects planets and their paths through the universe.

Albert Einstein won the Nobel Prize for physics. Since he was now famous he talked about things other than science that were of great interest and concern to him. He wanted the Jews to have a homeland in Palestine. Because of his opinion on this issue, the German government did not allow him back into Germany. He came to the United States and took a position at the Institute for Advanced Studies in Princeton, New Jersey.

In time, the world became engulfed in World War II. Albert wrote to President Franklin Roosevelt and told him that the United States should develop the atomic bomb before Hitler did. From his studies Albert knew how powerful the atom could be in producing an explosion. Later, he said that his letter was "the greatest mistake of my life."

Albert died of a heart problem in 1955. Until the day he died, he still was trying to answer questions he considered important.

1. What two words were most important in the biography of Albert Einstein? Why?
2. Who among your classmates (excluding yourself) is closest to becoming the next Albert Einstein? Why?
3. What do you think Albert meant when he wrote, "Something deeply hidden had to be behind things"?
4. What great unanswered question can you think of? Write it on a card and ask a family member to save it for you until you become an adult.

SOCIAL STUDIES

1. Look up these terms: *speed of light, gravity, mass, energy, space, time,* and *motion.* Choose one of these terms and try to explain it in words that are easy to understand.
2. In what year did Albert Einstein win the Nobel Prize for physics? What is physics? Would you ever want to study physics? Why or why not?
3. Why do you think Albert said that his letter to President Franklin D. Roosevelt about building the atomic bomb was "the greatest mistake of my life"? Do you think it was? Why or why not?

FURTHER READING

Goldenstern, Joyce. *Albert Einstein: Physicist and Genius.* Great Minds of Science Series. Springfield, NJ: Enslow Publishers, 1995.

Hammontree, Marie. *Albert Einstein: Young Thinker.* Childhood of Famous Americans Series. New York: Macmillan, 1986.

Reef, Catherine. *Albert Einstein: Scientist of the 20th Century.* Taking Part Books. New York: Silver Burdett, 1991.

ANNE FRANK ★ 1929–1945

Young Diarist, Victim of the Holocaust

Anne's father, Otto Frank, was an officer in the German army during World War I. His ancestors had lived in Frankfurt am Main, Germany, for hundreds of years. But now it was the 1930s and life was much different because Adolf Hitler was chancellor of Germany.

Even though Otto Frank and his family were Germans, they were also Jews. Because of Germany's anti-Jewish policies at the time, Jews lost their jobs and their stores were boycotted. Even Jewish books were burned. In 1933 the Frank family moved to Amsterdam, Holland; they felt much safer in another country. Mr. Frank was a partner in an import business, and he set up his factory in Holland.

But in 1940 Hitler invaded Holland. Jews were discriminated against in many ways. Dutch schools were closed to Jews, so Anne and her older sister Margot went to a Jewish secondary school.

On her thirteenth birthday Anne received a gift of blank book pages. She began a diary and called it "Kitty." This diary was found much later. It tells the story of what happened to Anne and her family.

Mr. Frank prepared a hiding place for his family and others in the upstairs rooms of his factory. They were destined to live there for the next two years.

Anne wrote that she thought it was odd keeping a diary. She was sure no one would be interested. "Still, what does it matter?" she wrote. "I want to write, but more than that, I want to bring out all kinds of things that lie buried deep in my heart." What came out of her heart and into her diary was a longing for friends and freedom, the distaste for the same kind of food each day, and how she was maturing as a person during the years of confinement.

Month after month went by. At night they were in fear that the Allied forces, unaware that they were in hiding, would drop bombs on them. During the day, they could not look out the attic window for fear someone on the street would see them. But the group of eight people listened to forbidden radio programs from England. They learned that the Allies were beginning to win the war. They also heard the bad news: Hitler was putting Jews in gas chambers and executing them.

After two years of hiding, they were betrayed by someone. Nazi soldiers came one day and put them under arrest. Anne's diary was thrown on the floor with the trash. At first they were all together in a camp in Holland. Then they were crammed into a freight car and sent to Auschwitz, a notorious death camp. Anne and Margot were separated from their parents and sent to the Bergen-Belsen camp, where they caught the disease of typhus. As prisoners, they were always hungry and thirsty. The two girls finally died.

Otto Frank was the only survivor of those who hid in the upper rooms of his factory. He went back after the war and was given the diary that his daughter Anne had written. It became a book, a play, and a powerful movie— a fitting remembrance of a brave young girl.

1. Anne Frank wrote in her diary, "Memories mean more to me than dresses." What does that sentence mean to you? What does it tell you about the kind of person Anne was and the life she had?

2. Anne wrote that writing in her diary brought ". . . out all kinds of things that lie buried deep in my heart." What do you think Anne meant by that statement? What do you think is the purpose of writing in a diary or journal?

3. Before reading Anne's diary, write several things that you think might have been on her mind. Then, as you read her diary, keep a reading journal of your own. Write down your thoughts and feelings in response to what Anne wrote.

4. Pretend you live on another planet and have just received Anne Frank's biography through a Planet Inter-Fax. What would you report to your people about Anne Frank's experience on planet Earth?

SOCIAL STUDIES

1. Find Amsterdam, Netherlands (Holland), on a map. What sea and countries border the Netherlands? Read about Amsterdam in a reference book. What interests you most about the city?

2. What rules are you required to follow? How do they compare to the ones Anne and her Jewish family and friends had to obey?

3. If you had to hide, as Anne did, what three things would you take with you to your hiding place?

4. What must nations and individuals do to ensure that humankind will never again experience such a horror as the Holocaust?

FURTHER READING

Abells, Chana Byers. *The Children We Remember*. New York: Greenwillow, 1986.

Adler, David A. *A Picture Book of Anne Frank*. New York: Holiday House, 1993.

Frank, Anne (translated from the Dutch by B. M. Mooyaart-Doubleday). *Anne Frank: The Diary of a Young Girl*. New York: Doubleday, 1967.

Meltzer, Milton. *Rescue: The Story of How Gentiles Saved Jews in the Holocaust*. New York: HarperCollins Children's Books, 1988.

MOHANDAS KARAMCHAND GANDHI ★ 1869–1948

Spiritual and Political Leader of India

When Mohandas was growing up, Indian parents chose wives for their sons. The arrangements were often made when children were quite young, sometimes six or seven years old. When Mohandas was thirteen, his parents chose a girl of his own age named Kasturbai Makanji. They were married while in school, and continued living with their own parents, as was the custom.

In 1888 Mohandas, known as Gandhi, went to England to study law, leaving his wife and baby in India. Gandhi respected the English, although he did not like their rule in India. In 1891, after passing his law exams in London, he returned home to his family.

Two years later, Gandhi took a job as a lawyer for one year in South Africa. Great Britain ruled there too. Gandhi was struck by the many kinds of discrimination nonwhites experienced in South Africa, where ninety thousand Indians lived. South Africans who were not white had to carry passes identifying themselves. The British did not consider any marriage legal unless it was Christian.

Such discrimination bothered Gandhi greatly. He returned to India and wrote articles about British discrimination against Indians in South Africa. Nevertheless, he took his wife and children back with him to South Africa, where he felt he could do some good. At that time Dutch farmers, called Boers, went to war with the British. Gandhi sided with the British and organized the Indian Volunteer Corps. The volunteers worked as stretcher bearers for the English troops and received the War Medal for their meritorious service.

In 1915 Gandhi and his growing family returned to India. No longer did he wear business suits that marked him as a prominent lawyer. He wore only Indian clothing. He traveled throughout India and was overwhelmed by the poverty, prejudice, unjust laws, and deplorable working conditions the people had to endure. Gandhi invented the word *satyagrapha*, which means "peaceful force" or "soul force." Courage, nonviolence, and truth—those were his ways to counteract prejudice and discrimination. He believed that people's behavior was more important than their position or class in life. An Indian poet, Rabindranath Tagore, called him *Mahatma*, meaning "saint" or "great soul." Gandhi was uncomfortable with the title, yet the world came to know him as Mahatma Gandhi.

In 1947 the British finally granted India its freedom. Then Muslims and Hindus in India fought each other. Gandhi fasted, eating nothing, until the two groups came to him in peace. Soon after, a Hindu fanatic shot Gandhi as he led a crowd in prayer. Gandhi's sons pleaded for the assassin's life, for they knew their father revered all life, even that of a person who would kill him.

Gandhi had written, "I cannot intentionally hurt anything that lives, much less fellow human beings, even though they may do the greatest wrong to me and mine." Gandhi served as an example to people around the world that a nonviolent approach to social wrongs can make a difference.

1. Write a paragraph about someone you know or have read about who has some of the same qualities as Gandhi. Be sure to include what those qualities are.
2. Write a response to Gandhi's statement, "I cannot intentionally hurt anything that lives, much less fellow human beings, even though they may do the greatest wrong to me and mine."
3. Could you plead for the life of a person who killed a relative or friend of yours? Why or why not?

SOCIAL STUDIES

1. Write a letter to Gandhi telling him your feelings about capital punishment. Are you for it or against it?
2. Find India and South Africa on a map or globe. Look in a reference book to find out what other countries were ruled by the British at one time or another. (Look under *British Empire, Great Britain,* or *United Kingdom.*)
3. Hold a class debate on the pros and cons of this statement: Parents should select their children's husbands and wives for them.

Ask parents for their opinions before you debate. Keep in mind that other cultures often have good reasons for customs that may seem strange to us.

FURTHER READING

Bush, Catherine. *Mohandas K. Gandhi.* World Leaders Past & Present Series. New York: Chelsea House Publishers, 1985.

Fisher, Leonard Everett. *Gandhi.* New York: Atheneum Books for Young Readers, 1995.

Lazo, Caroline. *Mahatma Gandhi.* Peacemakers Series. New York: Silver Burdett, 1993.

GEORGE WASHINGTON GOETHALS ★ 1858–1928

Civil Engineer and Army Officer

Growing up in New York City in the 1870s was a fascinating experience for George Goethals. The buildings seemed to reach to the sky. Young boys raced from one office to another carrying messages. George worked part-time as a messenger, saved his money, and went to the College of the City of New York. Before he graduated, he was appointed to the United States Military Academy at West Point, and by 1880, he was a second lieutenant in the Army Corps of Engineers.

George's first job was to build a 120-foot bridge. Since he had never built a bridge before, he read books on bridge building at night and supervised its construction during the day.

West Point asked him to come back and teach engineering courses. While there he met Effie, the sister of an officer friend. He and Effie were married in 1884 and were later the parents of two boys.

The peacetime Army Corps of Engineers planned and directed the dredging of rivers, the construction of flood-control works, and the finding of routes for railroads.

Many people in the United States realized how important a canal in Central America was to our military defense, for we needed a quick way to get ships from the Atlantic to the Pacific and back. It took battleships weeks to go around Cape Horn.

After the first American engineer asked to be relieved of building the Panama Canal, President Theodore Roosevelt appointed George to take complete charge of the project. The president also put Colonel W. C. Gorgas in charge of sanitation. Yellow fever and malaria had to be eliminated, for if the workers died, the canal could not be built. Colonel Gorgas got rid of the mosquitoes by having oil poured over stagnant waters where mosquito larvae grew. Swamp grass was burned, and the men slept under mosquito netting.

Meanwhile, George was working with the men. Their initial distrust turned to great admiration. They never knew when he would appear where they were working. Those who loafed soon lost their jobs. George worked six days a week. On Sundays he acted as judge in cases where canal workers felt they were not treated fairly.

George asked Harry F. Hodges to build the great locks that raise and lower the ships. There are forty-six pairs of gates, seventy-five feet wide. The locks raise and lower ships as high as four- to eight-story buildings.

Because landslides occurred often during construction, George was constantly in the field, helping and encouraging the men to keep working and not lose heart. The great Panama Canal opened only six years after he was put in charge, on September 26, 1913.

George returned home. During World War I, he took charge of the army's Quartermaster Department, arranging for American soldiers to get the food and equipment they needed. He never served as a combat soldier, but he did a great deal for his country while serving in the military.

1. What are the three most interesting facts in the biography of George Goethals?
2. Why would you trust George if you worked for him?
3. Create three titles for the biography of George Goethals. List them with your classmates' on the board and vote for the three best.

SOCIAL STUDIES

1. Have a class member stop by an Army Recruitment Center and ask a recruiter for information or a brochure on the Army Corps of Engineers. Discuss the information as a class. In times of war, what does the Army Corp of Engineers do? Of all these tasks, which one would you prefer to do? Why?
2. Read about the construction of the Panama Canal in a reference book. What job would you consider most interesting to do? Why?
3. What would happen if the Panama Canal had not been built? How do you think it would affect the United States financially? militarily? Trace around the tip of South America on a map or globe to get an idea about the added distance ships would travel if the Panama Canal were not available to them.
4. With a partner or small group, look up canals and locks in a reference book. Then draw a poster or build a model to show how a lock works.

FURTHER READING

Latham, Jean Lee. *George W. Goethals: Panama Canal Engineer*. Discovery Biographies Series. New York: Chelsea House, 1993.

MATTHEW HENSON ★ 1866–1955

Arctic Explorer

When Matthew Henson was very young, his parents moved from their small farm in Maryland to Georgetown, a village near Washington, D.C. They were African Americans and wanted to escape the violence that the Ku Klux Klan was brutally inflicting on African Americans after the Civil War.

Matthew was seven when his mother died. He then lived with an uncle, but by the time he was fourteen, his father had died and his uncle could no longer support him. So Matthew washed dishes in a restaurant and then decided to venture forth on his own. He walked forty miles to Baltimore and was hired as a cabin boy aboard Captain Childs's ship, the *Katie Hines*.

Captain Childs continued Matthew's education by teaching him geography, history, mathematics, and literature during the ship's long voyages. They sailed across the Pacific Ocean to China, Japan, and the Philippines. In the Atlantic they sailed to France, Africa, and the Arctic city of Murmansk, in Russia. The Captain died at sea, and Matthew, then nineteen, left the ship when it returned to the United States.

A job in a hatter's shop opened for Matthew. One day, a customer needed a hat to wear in Nicaragua. He was a United States naval officer named Robert E. Peary. The government was sending him to Nicaragua to search for a possible canal route across the Isthmus of Panama. He needed a servant to help him and he asked Matthew if he would be interested, and Matthew accepted.

Matthew's work in Nicaragua impressed Peary. He asked the twenty-one-year-old Matthew to explore Greenland and the North Pole regions with him. When Peary told him he had no money to pay him, Matthew laughed and said there would be no place to spend it at the North Pole.

Peary and Matthew made five trips to the far North. With each trip they came closer to their goal: to be the first to reach the North Pole. Matthew learned to speak the language of the Inuit people, build sledges, drive sled dogs, build igloos, and survive in weather fifty degrees and more below freezing. The Inuits called Matthew *Miy Paluk,* or "Dear Little Matthew."

In 1907 Matthew married Lucy Ross. The following year, he began his last trip to the Arctic with Peary. On April 6, 1909, Commander Peary, Matthew Henson, and four Inuits reached the North Pole—90° north latitude. Even so, not everyone believed they got there or that they were the first. After experts studied the records, the two Americans finally got credit for the discovery.

On his return to the United States, Matthew was in his early forties. He wrote his autobiography and took a job with the United States Customs Bureau. He worked there for twenty-eight years and retired in 1940.

Matthew died in 1955 and was buried in Woodlawn Cemetery in the Bronx, New York. Later he was disinterred and buried in Arlington National Cemetery beside Admiral Robert E. Peary and was recognized as the codiscoverer of the North Pole.

READING

1. Write an obituary for Matthew Henson. How will you title it?

2. Pretend you are in an igloo at the North Pole with Matthew Henson and you are waiting to travel. What would you and Matthew talk about? What questions would you ask him?

3. If you were a cabin boy or girl, as Matthew was, what countries would you want to visit? Why?

4. Why was it important for Matthew to be disinterred and buried next to Robert E. Peary?

SOCIAL STUDIES

1. On a map, find the places where Matthew traveled: China; Japan; the Philippines; France; Africa; Murmansk, Russia; Nicaragua; Greenland; and the North Pole. Read about them in a reference book. Of all these places, which would you prefer to visit? Why?

2. Read about Inuits in a reference book. Find out how they stay warm in their northern climate. As an Inuit boy or girl, what work do you think you would be required to do for your family?

3. What part of the world would you like to explore? Draw a picture of yourself there and give the picture a title.

4. How long are the summer days near the North Pole? How long is the longest day in your summer?

FURTHER READING

Ferris, Jeri. *Arctic Explorer: The Story of Matthew Henson*. Minneapolis: Carolrhoda Books, 1989.

Gilman, Michael. *Matthew Henson*. Black Americans of Achievement Series. New York: Chelsea House Publishers, 1988.

Haskins, Jim. *Against All Opposition: Black Explorers in America*. New York: Walker and Company, 1992.

_____. *One More River to Cross: The Story of Twelve Black Americans*. New York: Scholastic, 1992.

Williams, Jean. *Matthew Henson: Polar Adventurer*. New York: Franklin Watts, 1994.

DANIEL K. INOUYE ★ 1924–

United States Senator

The Inouye family was poor. Oftentimes, for breakfast, Daniel's mother prepared one hard-boiled egg for all of them by slicing it into six parts. The rest of the meal consisted of fruits gathered in the Hawaiian mountains, such as guavas, mangoes, mountain apples, and wild plums. They finished their meal with milk.

One night, Daniel was pleased to have chicken. There was enough for everyone. But when he went to find his pet chicken the next day, it was gone. His mother said, "We ate it at supper last night. And we all thank you for taking such good care of it until it was ready to eat."

Daniel wanted to be a surgeon, so he took a Red Cross first-aid course. On December 7, 1941, he had to put his learning to use, for the Japanese bombed the United States military base at Pearl Harbor, Hawaii. For five days Daniel helped those wounded in the bombardment.

As soon as he could, Daniel enlisted in the army and was sent to Mississippi to join the 442nd Regimental Combat Team made up of Japanese Americans. This regiment went to Italy to battle the Italian and German armies. Daniel was given a battlefield commission to second lieutenant. For his bravery and service, he received the Distinguished Service Cross, the Bronze Star, and the Purple Heart with two oak-leaf clusters (signifying that he was awarded two more Purple Hearts). But his right arm had been severely injured and had to be amputated. Tying his shoes, writing with his left hand, and driving were just a few things he had to relearn.

Daniel's dream of becoming a surgeon was out of the question, so he turned to the study of law. He took prelaw courses at the University of Hawaii, where he met Margaret (Maggie) Awamura, a speech instructor at the university. On their second date he asked her to marry him. She immediately said yes. Soon after his graduation they went to Washington, D.C., where Daniel enrolled in George Washington University law school. He received his J.D. degree in 1952.

Daniel passed his bar examination and took a job as assistant prosecutor for the city and county of Honolulu. He took politics seriously, for he wanted to become an elected official. Daniel knew the Democrats needed younger people in the party to give it new life.

He involved his veteran friends from World War II who were of Japanese, Portuguese, Caucasian, and Hawaiian descent. Many people told him that he was beating his head against a stone wall, for the Republicans had held power for a long time and were too strong politically to be defeated. But when Hawaii became a state in 1959, Daniel was the first Japanese American to serve in the U.S. House of Representatives. In 1962 he was elected to the Senate.

Since that time he has been reelected every term. Now he and his wife travel back and forth between Hawaii and Washington, D.C., and continue to devote themselves to public service.

1. What lesson did Daniel Inouye probably learn when his mother served his pet chicken for the family meal?

2. From your reading of the biography of Senator Inouye, what in his background would make you comfortable having him as your elected representative?

3. Write a letter from your class to Senator Inouye. Tell him what you admire about him from having read his biography and what more you would like to know about him. (You can also write to any other senator, congressman, or congresswoman you admire.)

4. Try writing your name with the hand you do not normally use. How does it compare with that of your writing hand?

SOCIAL STUDIES

1. Daniel received his J.D. degree from George Washington University. What is a J.D. degree? Ask a lawyer to visit your class and answer questions about law school.

2. How long may a member of the U.S. House of Representatives serve before seeking reelection? Who is the member of Congress from your district? If you do not know, how can you find out?

3. How long may a U.S. Senator serve before seeking reelection? Who is the senator from your district?

4. Find the Hawaiian Islands on a map. Approximately how far are they from the United States mainland? Read about Hawaii and share three interesting facts with the class.

FURTHER READING

Green, Carl R., and William R. Sanford. *The Congress*. American Government Series. Vero Beach, FL: The Rourke Corporation, Inc., 1990.

Johnston, Joyce. *Hawaii*. Hello U.S.A. Series. Minneapolis, MN: Lerner Group, 1995.

McNair, Sylvia. *Hawaii*. America the Beautiful Series. Chicago: Childrens Press, 1989.

Sinnott, Susan. *Extraordinary Asian Pacific Americans*. Chicago: Childrens Press, 1993.

Weber, Michael. *Our Congress*. I Know America Series. Brookfield, CT: The Millbrook Press, 1996.

Mahalia Jackson was born with an eye infection and bowed legs. Her mother Charity massaged her legs every night. Her father Johnny worked three jobs: daytime as a longshoreman on the New Orleans wharves, evenings at a barbershop, and weekends as a Baptist preacher. Charity died suddenly at age thirty, and the little girl and her brother went to live with her Aunt Duke.

Mahalia loved to sing. She joined the children's choir at the Plymouth Rock Baptist Church.

When she finished eighth grade, Mahalia quit school. She worked ten-hour days as a laundress in order to bring in money to support the family. Yet her Aunt Duke felt she could not handle fifteen-year-old Mahalia and sent her to live in Chicago with her Aunt Hannah.

When Hannah became ill, Mahalia, who had begun nurse's training, dropped out of school and took over her aunt's job as cook for a white family. She also did other housework duties, sang at churches, and joined local singing groups in the evenings and on weekends. Mahalia made $1.50 a night, which was a good wage at that time.

These were the Depression years, which were difficult for most persons but especially hard for African Americans. Mahalia worked as a maid in a hotel during the day and often sang gospel music at the same hotel in the evenings and weekends. Although she was offered a great deal of money to sing the blues, gospel songs were all she would sing.

Because her singing style made her popular, Mahalia had enough money to open a beauty salon and florist shop. Many of her African American fans came to have their hair set and buy flowers. She began making records and became nationally known for one special song titled, "Movin' on Up." It sold more than two million records. She took her gospel music from the churches to the concert stage of Carnegie Hall in New York City.

Racial intolerance concerned Mahalia. Even though white audiences were enthusiastic about her singing, she and her friends were often refused service at restaurants after her concerts. Gas station attendants would not sell them gas or oil. Many times Mahalia slept in her car at night because she could not get a room in a motel or hotel. When she bought a forty-thousand-dollar house in Chicago's suburbs, someone shot air-rifle pellets through her living-room window. She called the mayor of Chicago about her problems and he gave her police protection. When Edward R. Murrow, a famous newscaster, heard about the way she was being treated, he came to her house and interviewed her on his weekly "Person to Person" television program. After that, she was not harassed.

She joined with Martin Luther King, Jr., and Ralph David Abernathy, civil rights activists, and sang without pay at their fund-raising events. Mahalia toured Europe, Asia, and Japan singing her gospel songs until her health began to fail. She is remembered as the greatest gospel singer of the twentieth century.

1. Write Mahalia a letter about something she did or experienced. Exchange your letter with another student and answer his or her letter as if you were Mahalia.
2. With a group, write a song about Mahalia and perform it for the class.
3. What is the difference between gospel music and the blues? Why do you think Mahalia refused to sing the blues?
4. How did you feel when you read of the discrimination Mahalia Jackson experienced? Have you experienced discrimination because of your race, looks, size, or speech? How did you feel?

SOCIAL STUDIES

1. Find New Orleans and Chicago on a map. What states would you cross if you went straight from Chicago to New Orleans? Read about the two cities in a reference book. Which of the two sounds more interesting to you? Why?
2. Here are a few of the songs Mahalia sang: "It Is No Secret," "Walk in Jerusalem," "Move on up a Little Higher," "He's Got the Whole World in His Hands," "Joshua Fit the Battle of Jericho," "Sweet Little Jesus Boy," "The Holy City," "Nobody Knows the Trouble I've Seen," "Just a Closer Walk with Thee," and "I Believe." Get a recording of Mahalia singing and listen to it with the class. Then write a music review describing Mahalia's voice and what is special about her singing.
3. Mahalia sang without pay at fund-raising events to help people become aware of racial intolerance. What are some things you can do to ease racial divisions?
4. Read about gospel music in a reference book or a music textbook. List five things that are special about gospel music.

FURTHER READING

Donloe, Darlene. *Mahalia Jackson*. Los Angeles, CA: Holloway, 1992.

Dunham, Montrew. *Mahalia Jackson: Young Gospel Singer*. Childhood of Famous Americans Series. New York: Aladdin Paperbacks, 1995.

Gourse, Leslie. *Mahalia Jackson: Queen of Gospel Song*. Impact Biographies Series. New York: Franklin Watts, 1996.

Witter, Evelyn. *Mahalia Jackson: Born to Sing Gospel Music*. Milford, MI: Mott Media, Inc., 1985.

Wolfe, Charles K. *Mahalia Jackson*. American Women of Achievement Series. New York: Chelsea House Publishers, 1990.

HELEN KELLER ★ 1880–1968

Advocate for People with Impairments and Disabilities

At two years of age, Helen became very ill with fever and pain. The doctor came to her home in Tuscumbia, Alabama, but could not diagnose the problem. Helen's pain and fever eventually left her. Tragically, however, the sickness took away her sight and hearing, and she was thrust into a world of darkness and silence.

Helen's father contacted Dr. Alexander Graham Bell, the inventor of the telephone. With his help, Helen soon had a teacher named Annie Sullivan. Annie felt it best that she and Helen live alone in a cottage away from the house. The Kellers took Helen for a long drive and dropped her off at the cottage. Helen did not know that she was so close to home.

Annie forced Helen to behave so she could teach the child something. Finally Annie succeeded. Progress was slow, but the high point came when Annie and Helen stood beside a water pump. When the water spilled over Helen's hands, Annie slowly spelled the word *water* in Helen's wet, outstretched hand. Quickly, Helen got the connection. That cool liquid had a name! Everything had a name! Now Helen wanted to know everything.

Helen went from one object to another, touching each one. Annie spelled the word of each in Helen's hand. In a few weeks, Helen knew 300 words. The world of books burst upon Helen as she learned to read braille.

Helen went to school and then to college with Annie. She took courses in elementary Greek, advanced Latin, geometry, and algebra. A college official spelled out the final-exam questions in Helen's hand, and Helen typed the answers on a typewriter. She graduated with honors from Radcliffe College, the women's division of Harvard University.

In 1903 Helen and Annie wrote a book, *The Story of My Life*. Now the two of them had enough money to live very well, and they didn't have to depend on others for help.

Helen had a deep concern for people, and especially for women, the physically challenged, and the poor. She labored tirelessly to perfect her speech. She began lecture tours, and many people came to hear her words of hope for the disabled and poor. She even portrayed herself in a Hollywood movie called *Deliverance*. She was advertised as "the eighth wonder of the world."

During the 1930s Helen traveled all over the world urging people to care for those who had visual impairments. When World War II began, many young soldiers became disabled and blind from combat. Helen went to the hospitals to encourage them. Many of these men had read about Helen when they were in school. Now they got to know her personally. She even danced with them.

Helen lectured on every continent on Earth except Antarctica. Her many books were translated into more than fifty languages.

After World War II, Helen went to Japan to visit those who were burned in the atomic bomb blasts of Hiroshima and Nagasaki. Helen Keller spent her life encouraging people who were poor or deprived or who had disabilities.

READING

1. Why do you suppose that Helen Keller acted so wildly as a child? Write a paragraph on how she might have felt.
2. Why do you think it was significant for Helen to realize that things had names? What would your world be like without language?
3. Dramatize, with a friend, Annie and Helen at the water pump when Helen learns her first word.
4. Why was Helen advertised as "the eighth wonder of the world"?

SOCIAL STUDIES

1. Ask a person who has a hearing impairment (and a translator, if necessary) to visit your class to teach you some sign language. Prepare a set of questions to ask him or her about what it is like to have a hearing impairment.
2. Find Hiroshima and Nagasaki on a map of Japan. Read about them in a reference book. Why do you suppose Helen wanted to visit the people there?
3. Helen traveled to many continents. What kinds of obstacles would she have met in traveling from one continent to another?
4. Which of the two disabilities—blindness or deafness—would be the most difficult for you to live with? Why?

FURTHER READING

Davidson, Margaret. *Helen Keller*. New York: Scholastic, 1989.

Graff, Stewart and Polly Anne. *Helen Keller*. Discovery Biography Series. New York: Chelsea Juniors, 1992.

Lundell, Margo. *A Girl Named Helen Keller*. Hello Reader Series. New York: Scholastic, 1995.

MARTIN LUTHER KING, JR. ★ 1929–1968

Minister and Civil Rights Activist

Martin Luther King, Jr., learned at a young age that the color of one's skin made a difference to people. He could play with white friends in his backyard but not sit beside them on a bus, or in a movie, or at a lunch counter. He found this hard to understand.

When Martin turned fifteen, he entered Morehouse College in Atlanta, Georgia. At nineteen Martin felt he needed more education, so he went to Crozer Seminary in Pennsylvania for a master's degree. Crozer had mostly white students. There he learned about the Indian leader Mahatma Gandhi's nonviolent approach to social change.

From there Martin went to Boston University and entered its doctoral program. He met Coretta Scott in Boston and married her in 1953. That same year, he became the pastor of the Dexter Avenue Baptist Church in Montgomery, Alabama. The following year, he received his Ph.D. from Boston University.

In the South during the 1950s, African American children went to their own schools. There were separate drinking fountains and separate public toilet facilities. African Americans had to sit in the backs of buses and give up their seats if there was not enough room for a white person.

In Montgomery, Alabama, toward the end of 1955, an African American woman named Rosa Parks stepped onto a bus with her packages after a hard day's work. Rosa sat down in the black section of the bus. She refused to get up for a white person when the bus driver ordered her to move. Her arrest outraged Martin and led to his involvement in civil protest.

As the new African American preacher at the Dexter Avenue Church, Martin was voted by local leaders as chairperson of the boycott committee opposing the city bus system. Since he had just come to Montgomery, the local African American leaders thought it would be better for this newcomer to be the one to leave if the boycott was not effective.

But the boycott was successful, going on for over a year and costing many African Americans their jobs and resulting in some going to jail. The boycotters also had the inconvenience of walking to work or finding other kinds of transportation.

In 1960 Martin joined his father as copastor at the Ebenezer Baptist Church in Atlanta. In the years that followed, he and Coretta had four children. He led many racial protests, suffered in jail, and gave his famous "I Have a Dream" speech at the March on Washington, D.C., in 1963.

In 1964 he received the Nobel Prize for peace. He was thirty-five and the youngest person in history to receive the award.

Martin went to Memphis, Tennessee, in 1968 to help sanitation workers who were poorly paid, overworked, and without job security. While there, he was shot and killed.

Martin Luther King, Jr., was known for his nonviolent approach to social change. To honor him, Congress set aside the third Monday in January as a federal holiday.

1. Pretend you are sitting with Martin Luther King, Jr., on a bus the day after the Montgomery boycott ends. What questions would you ask him? What do you think he would say?

2. Read Martin Luther King's "I Have a Dream" speech in a reference book. Have a classmate or several classmates read it out loud to the class. Write down what you consider the most important phrase in the speech.

3. Among your relatives or friends, who is most like Martin Luther King, Jr.? In what ways?

4. Look up the Nobel Prize for peace in a reference book. Why do you think Martin won the Nobel Prize? Pretend you are in Oslo, Norway, to award the Prize to Martin. Write a short speech on why he deserves the award.

5. In Birmingham, Alabama, in 1963, African American children were among the people protesting nonviolently. Police turned hoses on them and let police dogs attack them. What cause would you support that would make you put up with such abuse?

SOCIAL STUDIES

1. What is a boycott? How is a boycott an example of nonviolent protest? What other kinds of nonviolent protest can you think of?

2. The local African American leaders in Montgomery, Alabama, chose Martin to head the boycott because he was new to their area. They thought that if the boycott did not work out, it would be easier for Martin to leave than for those who had lived there for a longer time. What do you think of that logic?

3. Read Martin's "I Have a Dream" speech in a reference book. What big dream about the future do you have? Make an outline of your dream speech and share your ideas with the class.

FURTHER READING

Adler, David A. *A Picture Book of Martin Luther King, Jr.* New York: Holiday House, 1989.

Altman, Susan. *Extraordinary Black Americans from Colonial to Contemporary Times.* Chicago: Childrens Press, 1989.

Darby, Jean. *Martin Luther King, Jr.* Minneapolis, MN: Lerner Group, 1990.

de Kay, James T. *Meet Martin Luther King, Jr.* Step-up Biographies Series. New York: Random House Books for Young Readers, 1989.

Faber, Doris and Harold. *Martin Luther King, Jr.* Tarrytown, NY: Marshall Cavendish, 1991.

Greene, Carol. *Martin Luther King, Jr.: A Man Who Changed Things.* Rookie Biography Series. Chicago: Childrens Press, 1989.

Jakoubek, Robert, *Martin Luther King, Jr.* Black Americans of Achievement Series. New York: Chelsea House Publishers, 1990.

Turner, Glennette Tilley. *Take a Walk in Their Shoes.* New York: Puffin Books, 1989.

Advice Columnist

Esther Pauline Friedman was born in Sioux City, Iowa, several minutes before her twin, Pauline Esther Friedman. The identical twins, inseparable throughout childhood and adolescence, were nicknamed "Eppie" and "Popo."

As they grew older, they both took violin lessons. When Eppie was not prepared, Popo would take her lesson first, walk out, and reenter as Eppie. The violin instructor never knew he had taught the same girl twice.

The idea of helping others was ingrained in them by observing their parents. When they were ten years old, they decided to bring some joy to the prisoners in the county jail. The sheriff thought it was fine, but he stayed close by while they played for the prisoners. They played their violins in hospitals, too, sometimes pretending they were children of patients.

The twins lived in Eau Claire, Wisconsin, for a few years. Eppie was involved in many service organizations, such as the Anti-Defamation League, the Gray Lady Corps, the Easter Seal Society, and the March of Dimes. She was particularly active in the National Council of Christians and Jews. Politics interested her as well. She became a staunch Democrat and was rising in the party when her husband, Jules Lederer had the opportunity for a major advancement with a company in Chicago.

Their daughter, Margo, was growing up and needed less care, so Eppie called the *Chicago Sun-Times* and asked if they needed help in reading the advice columnist's mail. Eppie learned that what they really needed was a writer for the column. The woman who had written the Ann Landers column had just died.

Using a rented typewriter, Eppie answered three sample letters. Her ability was evident, and when the editor of the newspaper called her, he said, "Good morning, Ann Landers. It's your column." The first day at work, five thousand letters were on Eppie's desk. Her first column was published on October 16, 1955.

For six months, Eppie was Ann Landers on a trial basis at the newspaper. She even persuaded Popo, who lived across the country, to help her for a short time. Eppie found that her contacts with many charitable organizations were of great help in answering the variety of problems that came across her desk. Soon she asked for assistance, and got it, because of the large volume of correspondence. Eppie insisted that every letter she received be answered. And the letters came in at a rate of more than thousand a day. As the years went on, she wrote a number of books and booklets that were helpful to both teenagers and adults.

By 1956, Popo and her husband had moved to San Francisco. Popo went to the *San Francisco Chronicle* and applied for their advice column job. She became the Dear Abby columnist.

Ann Landers gives advice every day to the thousands of people who read her column and write her letters. One can only imagine how many people she has helped over the years.

People of Purpose

1. Write a letter to Ann Landers and tell her what you admire about her.
2. Check in a reference book for the difference between fraternal and identical twins. What is the difference? How have Eppie and Popo acted like identical twins throughout their lives?
3. If Ann Landers came to visit your class, what kinds of questions would you want to ask her? What problems in your neighborhood or town would you like to discuss with her?

SOCIAL STUDIES

1. Find several of Ann Landers's columns in your local newspaper or at the library. Report to your class on a particular problem and the advice she gave. After reading a few of her columns, see if you can write a description of the kinds of advice she tends to give.
2. With a partner, write letters to each other asking advice for a specific problem. Then each of you pretend you are Ann Landers and answer each other's letter.
3. Find an advice column in a daily newspaper. Choose one person's problem and write a column advising him or her (from your own perspective) as to what he or she might do to resolve the problem. Ask a partner to do the same. Exchange answers with your partner and evaluate each other's advice.
4. What is a newspaper syndicate?

FURTHER READING

Gibbons, Agile. *Deadline! From News to Newspaper*. New York: HarperCollins Children's Books, 1987.

Granfield, Linda. *Extra! Extra! The Who, What, Where, When and Why of Newspapers*. New York: Orchard Books, 1994.

LYDIA LILIUOKALANI ★ 1838–1917

Queen of the Hawaiian Islands

Lydia's education prepared her to be queen of the Hawaiian Islands. At four years of age, she entered the Royal School, which was a boarding school managed by American missionaries to prepare future Hawaiian leaders. There she learned English and became proficient musically. She had perfect pitch and could sight-read musical scores.

Long before Lydia was born, the Hawaiian Islands were "discovered" in 1778 by Captain James Cook, a British naval explorer. People from other countries possibly had been there also, but if so, they had not recorded the fact.

Rapid changes came to the Hawaiian natives when Europeans settled there. The Hawaiian natives' immune systems could not ward off the diseases brought to the islands by people on foreign vessels. They caught whooping cough, measles, mumps, cholera, influenza, smallpox, and colds. These diseases spread rapidly through the population and many people died. Some of Lydia's siblings died of measles.

Numerous people from the United States came into Hawaii. They bought land to grow sugarcane and raise pineapples and other fruits. Thousands of workers from Japan came to work in the fields. Countries such as France, Spain, Great Britain, and particularly the United States were more than willing to take over the country as its "protectors." In reality, these countries wanted to annex Hawaii as their own. United States businessmen wanted Hawaii so they could send their products to the U.S. mainland.

The influence of the *haoles*, or Caucasians, became quite strong because the Hawaiian kings were politically weak leaders. When King David Kalakaua, Lydia's brother, died of kidney disease, Lydia, at fifty-one years of age, was next in line as ruler. The year was 1891.

Queen Liliuokalani decided now was the time to stop foreign investors, especially the American sugar planters, from gaining more power in the islands. One of her first acts was to appoint a new cabinet. Then she announced a new constitution. This document returned more power to the native Hawaiians, power given away by former Hawaiian kings.

But her cabinet ministers would not stand behind her. A small force of United States Marines came ashore pretending to protect U.S. citizens. A Committee of Safety came into power and declared the throne vacant, and Lydia was put under house arrest. She surrendered her government ". . . in order to avoid bloodshed," she said. Lydia also knew she could not fight a nation as strong as the United States.

A Honolulu-born American lawyer named Sanford B. Dole became governor. Within a half-century Hawaii was annexed to the United States and in 1959 became the fiftieth state.

Lydia left public life and wrote her autobiography and continued composing music. She wrote "Aloha Oe (Farewell to Thee)" and the Hawaiian National Anthem, "He Mele Lahui Hawaii." Her music and her concern for the well-being of native Hawaiians remain her lasting legacy.

1. Write three titles for Lydia Liliuokalani's biography. Compare your titles with a partner's and explain what you wrote.

2. Pretend that you are Queen Liliuokalani looking out upon the large number of U.S. troops and her small band of soldiers. Then complete this sentence: "If I were Queen Liliuokalani, I would . . . ."

_____

_____

_____

3. With a partner, write a song about Lydia's life and perform it for the class.

4. In a reference book, study the Hawaiian language. How many letters are in the Hawaiian alphabet versus the English alphabet? What meanings does the Hawaiian word *aloha* have? Learn some other Hawaiian terms and practice them with friends.

SOCIAL STUDIES

1. Read about Hawaii in a reference book. How many islands are in the Hawaiian chain? On which island would you prefer to live? Why?

2. One of the major social problems for the Hawaiians after foreign sailors came to their islands was illness from the diseases the sailors brought. If the Hawaiians could relive those years, what would or could they have done?

3. Why is the word *discovered* in quotation marks in this biography? Is it fair to say that Captain Cook "discovered" the Hawaiian Islands or that Columbus "discovered" America? Why or why not? Write a few sentences to answer these questions.

FURTHER READING

Johnston, Joyce. *Hawaii*. Hello U.S.A. Series. Minneapolis, MN: Lerner Publications Company, 1995.

Malone, Mary. *Liliuokalani, Queen of Hawaii*. Discovery Biographies Series. New York: Chelsea House, 1993.

McNair, Sylvia. *America the Beautiful: Hawaii*. America the Beautiful Series. Chicago: Childrens Press, 1990.

Sinnott, Susan. *Extraordinary Asian Pacific Americans*. Chicago: Childrens Press, 1993.

CHARLES A. LINDBERGH ★ 1902–1972

Aviator

Charles learned to drive a car when he was eleven years old. At fourteen, he drove his mother and uncle to California from their home in Minnesota. It took five weeks, for there were no superhighways at the beginning of the twentieth century. Charles's father trusted him. The year before, without any help, Charles had put together a new tractor his father had ordered for the farm.

When Charles arrived at college, he found it boring. He decided to take up flying. To pay for his lessons, he went on barnstorming trips with his instructor and worked as his mechanic and helper. He pulled the propeller to start the plane, and at fairs, he encouraged people to pay five dollars to go up in the plane with the instructor. To create interest, Charles even walked on the wings during flights so that more people came to watch and purchase tickets for rides.

In 1924 Charles enlisted as an Army Air Service Reserve pilot. Only 18 of the 104 men that began the program graduated. Charles was the best in the class.

Within two years, Charles was the chief pilot for a company that flew mail from St. Louis to Chicago. While flying the mail, he thought about making a nonstop, solo trip from New York to Paris. Someone had offered a twenty-five-thousand-dollar prize for the first person to make the flight. Charles thought he could do it by himself in a single-motor plane.

Charles had only two thousand dollars to spend on a plane, so some businesspeople in St. Louis backed him with their money. The plane, called *The Spirit of St. Louis,* was built in San Diego, California, and flown to New York. There, it was loaded with four hundred gallons of gasoline for the 3,600-mile flight. There was no radio because Charles had to keep the weight down in order to carry so much gasoline. He built a lightweight wicker seat on which to sit and refused one thousand dollars to carry a pound of mail for a stamp collector. Even so, he barely cleared a telephone wire at the end of the runway when taking off!

The night before he left, Charles did not sleep. In the sky he could not sleep either, for he had to be alert to control the airplane. At times he would open the window of the plane and let the cold air keep him awake. He crossed Nova Scotia, Newfoundland, the Atlantic Ocean, Ireland, and England, and arrived in Paris, France, 33-1/2 hours later.

Charles took his plane on a tour to each state in the United States. Then he visited Latin American countries as a goodwill ambassador. While in Mexico, he met and fell in love with the daughter of the U.S. ambassador, Anne Spencer Morrow. After they were married, he taught her how to fly. She later became known for her writing and her paintings. They had a baby boy who, sadly, was kidnapped and murdered. Because of their lack of privacy in the United States, they moved to England for a few years.

Charles's lifelong dedication to flying has made him a symbol of what is best in aviation. *The Spirit of St. Louis* hangs in the National Air and Space Museum in Washington, D.C.

1. Write a short newspaper article announcing Charles Lindbergh's arrival in Paris, France. Don't forget your headline.
2. Choose an event from Charles's biography and draw a picture of it. Give your picture a title.
3. Would you have refused to take a pound of mail for one thousand dollars across the Atlantic, as Charles did? Why or why not?
4. If Charles were here to take you any place in the world in his airplane, where would you ask him to take you? Why? What would you talk about along the way?

SOCIAL STUDIES

1. On a globe, trace Charles's flight from New York City to Paris, France. Why do you think he chose this route? With a partner, draw a poster showing the route for this famous flight.
2. Charles and his wife suffered from being so famous. What are some good and bad things about being famous? Which would you prefer, being famous or living a private life?
3. In a reference book, find a list of aviation records. Choose one to learn more about and give a report to the class.
4. Compare Charles Lindbergh with Amelia Earhart. How are they alike and different?

FURTHER READING

Burleigh, Robert. *Flight: The Journey of Charles Lindbergh*. New York: Philomel Books, 1991.

Demarest, Chris L. *Lindbergh*. New York: Crown Books for Young Readers, 1993.

Denenberg, Barry. *An American Hero: The True Story of Charles A. Lindbergh*. New York: Scholastic, 1996.

Juliette Gordon got her nickname soon after birth, when her uncle looked at her and exclaimed, "I'll bet she'll be a daisy!" The name stuck. She was "Daisy" from then on.

When she was older, Daisy rescued a child from drowning. Daisy's mother learned about it when she saw her daughter's wet clothes. Daisy kept quiet about the whole episode.

After graduation from Charbonnier's School for Girls, a finishing school in New York, Daisy's parents sent her to Europe. There she met William "Billow" Low through former friends in Savannah. They were married.

At their wedding, as the couple made their way through the many wedding guests, a grain of rice stuck in her good ear (she had only partial hearing in the other ear). Infection set in and she lost total hearing in that ear. Her married life began with only partial hearing in one ear.

Daisy and Billow spent time in England, Scotland, and the United States. She learned to paint, sculpt, and even do blacksmithing, for she was interested in everything and everyone around her.

In 1905, when they had been married less than twenty years, Daisy's husband died. Daisy did many things to keep busy after the loss of her husband. She went flying with English author Rudyard Kipling and became one of the first women to fly in an airplane. But her accomplishments did not relieve the emptiness she felt inside.

Then she met Robert Baden-Powell, the founder of the Boy Scouts. Like Daisy, he was a sculptor. He encouraged her to start a Girl Guides group in her Scotland home. Girl Guides is a program of personal enrichment and service to others. Daisy began with seven girls and a renewed sense of purpose in her life. She took them hiking and taught them how to sew. In London she started two more groups of Girl Guides. Back in Savannah, Daisy began more troops for girls. Then she traveled all over the United States and organized even more.

Daisy talked about her organization at every opportunity. With her hearing loss, she said she talked a lot because it was easier than trying to hear what people said to her. By 1913 the Girl Guides in the United States had become the Girl Scouts of America.

Daisy spent eighteen years traveling around the United States encouraging people to get involved in Girl Scouting. Daisy stepped down from the presidency of the Girl Scouts in 1920. By then there were forty thousand girls in scouting. The organization gave Daisy the title of *Founder*.

In 1927 Daisy died in the city where she was born, Savannah. A Liberty ship, called the *S.S. Juliette Low,* was launched eighteen years after her death. Four years later the Postal Service issued a stamp in her honor, and in 1983 a federal office building named for her was opened in Savannah, Georgia.

Daisy Low, a woman nearly deaf and often in poor health, wanted to make a difference in this world. And she did—especially in the lives of millions of young women.

1. Would you keep it a secret if you saved someone from drowning? Why or why not? Why do you think Daisy Low did?
2. List five admirable traits that Daisy had. Choose one that you would like to have in yourself and discuss with a classmate some practical steps you can take to develop that trait.
3. Daisy attended a finishing school. What kind of school was it? How do you think her education influenced what she did later?

4. Write a dialogue between Daisy and Baden-Powell about the goals of scouting. What would they say to each other?

SOCIAL STUDIES

1. Find Savannah, Georgia, on a map and in an encyclopedia. What body of water forms its eastern boundary? Read about the city and share two interesting facts with the class.
2. What are the goals of the Girl Scouts? What kinds of activities do Girl Scouts do? Have a Girl Scout explain the organization to the class.
3. Discuss in class how the Girl Scout Law could be adapted to apply to anyone.

The Girl Scout Law in the United States
I will do my best to be
    honest and fair
    friendly and helpful

considerate and caring
courageous and strong, and
responsible for what I say and do,
and to
    respect myself and others,
    respect authority,
    use resources wisely,
    make the world a better place, and
    be a sister to every girl scout.

"GIRL SCOUT LAW" FROM GIRL SCOUTS OF THE UNITED STATES OF AMERICA. REPRINTED BY PERMISSION.

4. How are the Girl Scouts and Boy Scouts alike and different?

FURTHER READING

Steelsmith, Shari. *Juliette Gordon Low: Founder of the Girl Scouts.* Biographies for Young Children Series. Seattle, WA: Parenting Press, Inc., 1990.

DOLLEY PAYNE MADISON ★ 1768–1849

Presidential Host and First Lady

Dolley loved the bright colors of the flowering countryside and pretty things such as jewelry and flowing dresses. Yet since she and her family were Quakers, she wore the plain clothes of the women of that faith. Her grandmother was not Quaker, so Grandmother Payne gave Dolley a pin to wear underneath her dress. When she lost it, Dolley thought God was punishing her for being vain.

Dolley was very attractive and many men were drawn to her. An interested suitor was James Madison, one of the writers of the Constitution. He asked for permission to visit her. Although Dolley was seventeen years younger than James, he proposed marriage. Dolley knew that if she married James, she would no longer be accepted as a member in the Society of Friends (another name for Quakers) because he was not of the same faith. Dolley decided to marry James anyway.

Martha Washington gave Friday socials that Dolley attended. Dolley enjoyed them, and everyone enjoyed Dolley's outgoing personality. When Thomas Jefferson was elected president, he appointed James Madison as his secretary of state. Since Jefferson's wife had died, he asked Dolley to be his host at the President's House. She quickly agreed and saw that delicious meals were prepared and that the guests had a good time, even though they differed politically from each other.

When James became president in 1809, Dolley continued as host with the title "Lady Presidentress." She decorated the President's House and had portraits of the first three presidents hung on the walls. At mealtime, American dishes such as fried chicken, New England clam chowder, and ice cream were served.

James led the United States into war with England because of their interference with American shipping. As a result, the English determined to invade the capital itself.

While James was with the troops, Dolley was gathering everything she could from the President's House. She saved the Declaration of Independence, the Constitution, silverware, and draperies. Just before she left, she took down the portrait of George Washington. When she found out that the frame made it too difficult to handle, she had the picture cut out. She left moments before the British troops came marching into the city. The soldiers burned the President's House but ate the meal Dolley had prepared for her family.

The war came to an end, and James finished his term of office. Dolley started a tradition for the children in Washington, D.C.: the Easter Egg Roll on the president's lawn. She helped orphans in the city, as well. Presidents' wives have continued their involvement in special projects, following the tradition Dolley started.

The Madisons retired to Montpelier in Virginia. After James died, Dolley returned to Washington, D.C. When she passed away, President Tyler called her the "First Lady for a half-century." A president's wife has been called "First Lady" ever since.

1. Going to Martha Washington's socials helped Dolley Madison to prepare for the time when she became host in the President's House. Make a list of the things that you think made Dolley Madison such an excellent host.
2. If you were to have a class party, who would you choose as your host? Why? What social traits and abilities does he or she have? Which ones would you like to have?
3. List two admirable or heroic things that Dolley did. What more would you like to know about them?

4. Why do you think Dolley moved from Virginia and went back to Washington, D.C., after her husband died?

SOCIAL STUDIES

1. In what year did the President's House become officially known as the *White House?* Search a reference book for the answer. Which president authorized the name *White House?*
2. Who is First Lady in the White House now? What project is she noted for?
3. How has the role of First Lady stayed the same since Dolley Madison's time? How has it changed?
4. If a woman were elected president, what role do you think her husband would serve? What would we call him?

FURTHER READING

Davidson, Mary R. *Dolley Madison: Famous First Lady*. Discovery Biographies Series. New York: Chelsea Juniors, 1992.

Klingel, Cindy. *Dolley Madison: Beloved First Lady (1768–1894)*. We the People Series. Mankato, MN: Creative Education, 1988.

NELSON ROLIHLAHLA MANDELA ★ 1918–

South African Black Political Leader

Nelson grew up in South Africa as a member of the Thembu tribe, of which his father, Henry, was a prominent leader. Nelson was a respectful, obedient son, even though his tribal middle name meant "stirring up trouble" or "bring trouble upon oneself."

Nelson was schooled by missionaries and learned to read and write English well. His family was very poor—so poor that Nelson had to wear his father's old clothes. His father died when Nelson was twelve, but before he died, he sent for the chief of the Thembu tribe and asked the chief to give Nelson an education and care for him. The chief agreed to do so. Nelson grew to a height of 6' 4", and he did well in boxing and long-distance running.

The white government of South Africa permitted only white legislators to serve, even though the vast majority of people were of black ancestry. The members of government passed laws that allowed only white people to vote. African men had to have an identity card (pass) to travel anywhere; if they did not have one, they would face possible time in prison. These and other laws were part of the South African system of *apartheid,* or "apartness."

In fear of potential black uprisings, the South African government banned any meetings of black Africans where more than three people planned to gather. On the night of December 4, 1956, police arrested Nelson for treason, along with 136 men and 19 women. Those arrested were black, colored (a mixture of black and white), and Indian and included a number of white people who were against apartheid. The trial lasted 4-1/2 years, but the government could not prove a communist conspiracy, because there wasn't any.

Nelson was convinced that nonviolence would not change the South African government's policies. Government officials were determined to put Nelson in jail, so he went underground with his organization, wearing different disguises and moving quietly from one place to another. He was eventually discovered and sentenced to prison for life on new charges.

While in prison, Nelson became a symbol of the injustice of apartheid. Over the years, many people and foreign governments appealed to the South African government through the "Free Mandela" campaign to let Nelson go. After having been imprisoned for nearly thirty years, Nelson was released in 1990.

Within a few years Nelson Mandela, by then in his mid-seventies, was elected president of South Africa. This election was the first one for the black majority in South Africa. The new government abolished apartheid and began a program of reconstruction and development. It started policies to improve mutual understanding and tolerance among the country's diverse ethnic and political groups. After much suffering and labor, Nelson's dreams for a peaceful, just South Africa have begun to come true.

1. How do you think Nelson Mandela lived up to the meaning of his tribal middle name? Why was it necessary for him to do so?
2. What do you think was the most difficult thing Nelson had to endure?
3. What was unjust about the policies of the South African government?
4. What would you do if the police did not permit more than three of your friends to meet with you? What organizations would you have to abandon?

SOCIAL STUDIES

1. Find South Africa on a map or globe. What countries border it? Choose one of these to read about in a reference book, and share a few facts with your classmates about what you learned.
2. Read about South Africa in a reference book. Find out who the minority whites are and where they came from. How did they gain control in the past?
3. Read in a newspaper, magazine, textbook, or reference book about the present situation in South Africa. What changes are taking place?
4. As a class, write Nelson Mandela a letter telling him what you admire about him and the changes he has brought to his country.

FURTHER READING

Dell, Pamela. *Nelson Mandela: Freedom for South Africa*. Picture Story Biographies. Chicago: Childrens Press, 1994.

Denenberg, Barry. *Nelson Mandela: "No Easy Walk to Freedom."* New York: Scholastic, 1991.

Hargrove, Jim. *Nelson Mandela: South Africa's Silent Voice of Protest*. People of Distinction Series. Chicago: Childrens Press, 1989.

Hughes, Libby. *Nelson Mandela: Voice of Freedom*. People in Focus Series. Parsippany, NJ: Silver Burdett, 1992.

THURGOOD MARSHALL ★ 1908–1993

Supreme Court Justice

Thurgood's name at birth was Thoroughgood, which was the name of one of his grandfathers. In elementary school, he changed his name to the shorter, easier version.

By the time Thurgood was in high school, he was over six feet tall and weighed nearly two hundred pounds. Since he was too big and strong to get a spanking for misconduct, the principal sent him to the furnace room with a copy of the United States Constitution. He memorized the whole document before he graduated.

Thurgood's mother Norma, a teacher, wanted him to become a dentist. When he graduated from high school, Thurgood went to Lincoln University in Oxford, Pennsylvania. His mother pawned her engagement and wedding rings to pay his tuition.

Thurgood became a member of the debate team. Dentistry, with its promise of good money, no longer interested him. He decided to study law. From Lincoln University, he went on to study at Howard University Law School in Washington, D.C. He realized that his mission in life was to help poor African Americans and disadvantaged people obtain their civil rights. Many of his clients could not pay for his services, but he helped them anyway.

Thurgood's secretary said he had a genius for accepting cases where he would not get a fee. He would remark, "Isn't it nice no one cares which twenty-three hours I work?" In 1936 Thurgood began his work as counsel to the National Association for Advancement of Colored People (NAACP).

Back in 1896, a case called *Plessy v. Ferguson* had come before the Supreme Court. The case concerned an African American man named Plessy who had refused to move from a section of a train reserved for white people only. A detective, Ferguson, arrested him for not moving to the blacks-only section. The Supreme Court ruled that separate but equal facilities did not violate the Constitution. Problems developed when the facilities for African Americans were not as good as those for white people.

Thurgood argued fifteen cases in front of the Supreme Court and lost only two. Then he took a case that challenged the *Plessy v. Ferguson* decision: It was called *Brown v. Board of Education of Topeka*. Seven-year-old Linda Brown had to cross railroad tracks every day to catch a bus to an African American school. A white school was closer to her home. Thurgood argued that separate schools for African Americans and whites was wrong. In 1954 the Supreme Court ruled in Thurgood's favor. The court said "separate but equal has no place" in the United States. As a result, people, despite their color, could sit in buses where they pleased and also go to schools near their homes.

Then in 1965 President Johnson made Thurgood Solicitor General and two years later appointed him to the United States Supreme Court. He was the first African American ever to hold such a position. He served on the Supreme Court until his retirement in 1991.

1. What were some of the personal characteristics of Thurgood Marshall that made him successful?
2. What two sentences in Thurgood's biography are most important to you? Why?
3. What did Thurgood mean when he said, "Isn't it nice no one cares which twenty-three hours I work"? How many hours do your parents work during an average day?
4. Write this beginning statement: "I will not forget . . ." Then write three sentences about Thurgood Marshall.

SOCIAL STUDIES

1. With a partner, pretend that you are Thurgood Marshall and your partner is a Supreme Court justice. Argue the case for Linda Brown in front of the justice. He or she will rule according to how well you argued your case. Then switch roles.
2. Stage a class debate. One side will argue for the segregation of schools and the other will argue for the integration of schools in the United States.
3. Does a person who cannot pay for a lawyer's advice or help have a right to free advice and help? Why or why not?

4. Make a list of some social issues you think are important enough to fight for. Exchange lists with classmates and discuss them.

FURTHER READING

Greene, Carol. *Thurgood Marshall: First African-American Supreme Court Justice*. Rookie Biography Series. Chicago: Childrens Press, 1991.

Haskins, James. *Thurgood Marshall: A Life for Justice*. New York: Henry Holt and Company, 1992.

Hess, Debra. *Thurgood Marshall: The Fight for Equal Justice*. History of the Civil Rights Movement Series. Englewood Cliffs, NJ: Silver Burdett Press, 1990.

Kronenwetter, Michael. *The Supreme Court of the United States*. American Government in Action Series. Springfield, NJ: Enslow Publishers, 1996.

Stein, R. Conrad. *The Bill of Rights*. Cornerstones of Freedom Series. Chicago: Childrens Press, 1992.

GOLDA MEIR ★ 1898–1978

Prime Minister of Israel

Golda patted the mud into a loaf of bread. She began to speak to her playmate when she felt the ground thumping underneath her knees. Hoofbeats! Horses ridden wildly by the Czar's cavalry—the cruel Russian Cossacks! There was no time for the two girls to run or find a place to hide. Golda and her friend fell flat into the mud and the troops laughed as they jumped their horses over them.

Life as a Jew was difficult in Russia during the early 1900s. The dreaded *pogroms* (organized attacks on minorities) allowed mobs to cause riots and kill Jews while the police looked the other way. Jews died for no reason other than the fact that they were Jewish.

Golda's father, Moshe, went to Milwaukee, Wisconsin, to earn money so he could bring his family to the United States. But he made only three dollars a week as a carpenter. There was not only his wife, Bluma, to bring to the United States but also his three little girls. After some time, Bluma decided the family could not live apart any longer. She started a bakery business in Pinsk (in southern Belarus or Belorussia) to make more travel money.

They boarded a small ship at Antwerp, Belgium, and finally were safely settled in the United States. Golda graduated from high school and went on to a teachers college, even though her parents thought she should marry Morris Myerson and raise a family. Later, Golda married Morris, who was shy and reserved and the opposite of sociable and lively Golda.

World War I brought more troubles for Jews all over Europe and elsewhere. They often lost their homes and were killed. Many of them wanted a homeland for themselves. Golda made speeches in synagogues, auditoriums, and on street corners, telling all who would listen about the plight of the Jews around the world. Her father was upset when he heard she was out on the street making speeches. He told her he would drag her home by her hair if he found her doing that again. But when he heard her one evening, he was thrilled with what she had to say and did not attempt to stop her. Golda spoke from her heart, without notes. She continued doing this the rest of her life.

In 1921 Golda and Morris left the United States and went to Palestine, where they first worked on a *kibbutz* (a collective farm). They planted trees, picked almonds, and farmed.

In the 1930s Hitler's Nazi soldiers in Germany forced Jews into concentration camps and killed them. Golda campaigned to have Jews sent to Palestine. She came back to the U.S. to raise money for the beginning of the new state of Israel. The money was used to build the Israeli army and to construct homes for Israel's new arrivals. Then on May 14, 1948, Israel became a country.

Golda held different positions in this new country, but the most important was that of prime minister. In 1956 she changed her name from Meyerson to Meir, meaning "to give light." She gave her country light until the time of her death in 1978.

1. For exactly five minutes, without stopping, write what you know about Golda. Do not stop to make corrections. Read what you wrote to a friend, and then listen to what he or she wrote. How are your papers alike and different?

2. Golda made speeches on street corners, telling of the abuses Jews experienced around the world. What does that tell you about her?

3. Have you experienced a narrow escape in your life? Write about it or draw a picture. How does it compare to Golda's experience with the horses and the Cossacks?

4. What does "to give light" mean to you? Is this something you can do? How?

SOCIAL STUDIES

1. Trace Golda's travels from childhood to adulthood on a map: Pinsk, Belarus (then Belorussia); Antwerp, Belgium; New York City; Milwaukee, Wisconsin; Israel (then Palestine). Read about Israel in a reference book and report three interesting things to your classmates.

2. Look up *kibbutz* (plural: *kibbutzim*) in a reference book. With a small group, discuss what you learned. If your group went to live on a kibbutz, what would your lives be like? Would you enjoy it?

3. Being prime minister of Israel is comparable to being president of the United States. When do you predict a woman will become president of the United States? What kind of woman would do the job best?

FURTHER READING

Adler, David A. *Our Golda: The Story of Golda Meir*. New York: Puffin Books, 1986.
Jacobs, William Jay. *Great Lives: World Government*. Great Lives Series. New York: Simon & Schuster Children's Books, 1992.

PATSY TAKEMOTO MINK ★ 1927–

United States Congresswoman

Little Patsy Takemoto constantly chased after her brother, Eugene, on the island of Maui. He was five-and-a-half years old and going to school across the road from their home. Patsy was only four but saw no reason why she could not be with him. The teacher and Patsy's parents laughed and did not object when she appeared at school with her brother. Before long Patsy was learning everything her brother learned, so she continued going to school. Learning became a lifelong process for Patsy, and she enjoyed every moment of it.

On December 6, 1941, Patsy turned fourteen. The next day, her life changed drastically, for Japanese bombers killed nearly 3,700 people. Most of those killed were U.S. Navy men at the Pearl Harbor Naval Base; others were people who lived in Hawaii and worked at the base. Patsy's family, as well as thirty-seven percent of the islands' population, was of Japanese descent.

Patsy entered the University of Hawaii after graduating from high school. She wanted to go to medical school in the United States, so she transferred to a school in Pennsylvania and later to the University of Nebraska. There she was assigned a room at the university's International House. Patsy soon learned that it was reserved for students who were not of white ancestry. She was indignant at being segregated and promptly sent off a letter to the local newspaper. The student body at the university became upset too, and soon all the dormitories were opened to all races.

Because of illness, Patsy had to finish her college degree in Hawaii. When she graduated,

she applied to the University of Chicago law school, where she met her future husband, John Mink. He was majoring in geology. They married in the campus chapel and later moved to Hawaii, where Wendy, their only child, was born. After the birth, Patsy opened a law office.

Patsy was a fine organizer and joined the Democratic party. She decided to run for office, and John became her campaign manager. Patsy spent twelve years as congresswoman in Washington, D.C.

She and John made a fine team. He directed all her campaigns while continuing to work in his field of geology.

During her terms in Congress, Patsy opposed war in Vietnam. She believed that the money pouring into the war effort could be better used to help the needy at home. She worked on many issues that came before the House of Representatives: nuclear testing, busing, school lunch programs, bilingual education, education for handicapped persons, and environmental protection.

In 1977 Patsy was appointed assistant secretary for Oceans and Environmental and Scientific Affairs by President Jimmy Carter. She resigned in 1978 and went home to Hawaii.

In 1990 her husband encouraged her to enter the race for the House of Representatives again, after so many years away from Washington. She entered and won! Patsy continues to work for the American people in the United States Congress, particularly on issues related to women, family and medical leave, and health care.

1. At the time this biography was written, Patsy Mink was a member of the House of Representatives from Hawaii. What might you predict for the future for Patsy?
2. Learning has been a lifelong process for Patsy. How do you think that has helped her? Why is it necessary to continue a lifetime of learning?
3. Reread the paragraph about the various issues that came before the House of Representatives while Patsy was there. Which issue is most important to you? Why? Explain your position in a short essay or speech.

SOCIAL STUDIES

1. How often are elections held for the House of Representatives?
2. How many members are there in the House of Representatives?
3. Some members of Congress are in office for many years. In your opinion, how long should a congressman or congresswoman be allowed to serve? Give two reasons for your answer.
4. How many women are in the House of Representatives? How many are in the Senate? Think of three reasons why more women should be members of Congress, either as representatives or senators. Write a newspaper editorial, using your three reasons as the basis for your argument.

FURTHER READING

Johnston, Joyce. *Hawaii*. Hello U.S.A. Series. Minneapolis, MN: Lerner Publications Company, 1995.

McNair, Sylvia. *Hawaii*. America the Beautiful Series. Chicago: Childrens Press, 1990.

Sinnott, Susan. *Extraordinary Asian Pacific Americans*. Chicago: Childrens Press, 1993.

MARIA MITCHELL ★ 1818–1889

Astronomer

The Mitchells had nine children running and playing around their house on Nantucket Island. William Mitchell, Maria's father, would joke to his wife, "Send home the neighbor children and bring ours into the house." She would answer in her Quaker speech, "Thee knowest they are all ours."

Mary thought her father was the best teacher that ever lived. He encouraged her to ask questions. As an astronomer, he took her to the roof of their home at night and taught her about the stars and planets in the sky. By the time she was four, Maria could read. A few years later she could set chronometers, clocks used on ships to determine the location at sea.

At the age of sixteen, Maria was a teaching assistant in a local school. When her father lost money on a business deal and the family needed financial support, Maria opened her own school. She advertised in the paper for girls aged six and older. They paid at least one cent a day, if they had the money. Maria's classes were different, for the whole world was her classroom. The children sometimes met early in the morning or late in the evening. Maria drew maps in the sand to show where countries were located on the earth. The girls learned about the heavens by using the telescope.

Maria's father found a job as cashier at the Pacific Bank in town. It not only paid well, but the bank provided the family with living quarters. Maria had her own room. There was also an observatory on the roof. She used her telescope for the United States Coast Survey.

Maria was a town librarian by day and an observer of the skies by night.

In 1847, while the Mitchells were having a party, Maria went to the roof to look through the telescope. To her amazement, she saw a light she had not seen before in one area of the sky. She rushed down and whispered in her father's ear. When he looked through the telescope, he told her she had sighted a comet. They recorded the coordinates—that is, where the comet was in the sky—and sent the information to astronomers. The king of Denmark had offered a gold medal to the first person to sight a "telescopic comet." Maria was the first to have seen it.

A wealthy general asked Maria to escort his daughter throughout the southern United States and Europe, offering to pay her way. Maria and the girl went down the Mississippi to New Orleans and then to England, where they visited Greenwich Observatory, which is located at zero degrees longitude. From there they went to Paris and Rome. In Rome Maria received special permission to visit the Vatican Observatory where Galileo had determined that the planets revolved around the sun.

On her return Maria was offered the position of professor of astronomy at Vassar, a new college for women. The girls at the college loved her, for she took them out of the classroom to view what the heavens were really like. She encouraged young women to take charge of both their present circumstances and their futures—to reach for the stars.

106

1. Maria Mitchell once said, "I was born of only ordinary capacity, but of extraordinary persistency." What did she mean? How does it explain her achievements? Does the statement describe you?
2. Why was Maria a good teacher? Other than your present teachers at school, who has been your best teacher? What does that person do that makes him or her so special?
3. Maria admired the early scientist Galileo. Read about Galileo's contributions to humankind. Why do you think Maria admired him so much?

4. What do astronomers do? Write a paragraph telling why you would want or not want to be an astronomer.

_____
_____
_____
_____

SOCIAL STUDIES

1. Trace Maria's route on a map as she escorted the wealthy general's daughter down the Mississippi to New Orleans and then to England, Paris, and Rome. What part of the trip would you have found most interesting?
2. In an encyclopedia, read about the Greenwich Observatory on the Thames River in England. Report to your classmates three things of interest.
3. Which way do the imaginary lines of latitude circle the Earth? Which way do the imaginary lines of longitude circle the Earth?
4. Read about Halley's comet in a reference book. According to astronomers, when is it due to pass the Earth again?

FURTHER READING

Camp, Carole Ann. *American Astronomers: Searchers and Wonderers*. Springfield, NJ: Enslow Publishers, 1996.

McPherson, Stephanie Sammartino. *Rooftop Astronomer: A Story About Maria Mitchell*. Minneapolis: Carolrhoda Books, 1990.

Stille, Darlene R. *Extraordinary Women Scientists*. Chicago: Childrens Press, 1995.

JULIA MORGAN ★ 1872–1957

Architect

As a child, Julia was a tomboy. She exercised on her brothers' athletic equipment in the barn and thought that the barn was a wonderful place to climb and play and swing on ropes. Even though she had frequent earaches and was small for her age, she was always ready to keep up with the boys.

Julia and her family lived in a large, three-story Victorian home in Oakland, California, just across the bay from San Francisco. The family was comfortably wealthy, but Julia and her brothers and sisters still had chores to do. Julia's responsibility was to polish and wax the banisters in their house.

Julia enrolled at the University of California and became the first woman student in the university's College of Engineering. The thought of becoming an architect consumed her, and the curriculum in engineering there included courses in architecture.

One of the young professors influenced Julia to go to the school in France where he had gone, the École des Beaux Arts of Paris. After three attempts Julia passed the entrance examination. Four years later, she was the first woman to graduate from its Architecture Section.

While in France, Julia met Phoebe Hearst. Phoebe's husband was a former United States senator and multimillionaire. Phoebe liked Julia and asked John Galen Howard to hire Julia to work in his architectural firm in San Francisco. Phoebe brought work to Julia. One assignment was to design a Greek theater seating six thousand people on the University of California campus. This was the first classi-cal open-air theater in the United States. Julia made it of reinforced concrete poured over steel rods, a technique she learned while in France and England.

Julia took the California state examination for architects and passed, becoming the first woman in the state to receive an architect's license. She decided to set up her own office.

In 1906 San Francisco experienced a devastating earthquake. The luxurious Fairmont Hotel was in shambles. Maria was asked to be the architect of a new Fairmont Hotel. The owners had heard of her work with reinforced concrete and were impressed when they heard that her buildings had survived the earthquake better than others.

After World War I Julia worked for Phoebe's son, William Randolph Hearst. William's 250,000-acre estate in San Simeon, California, was located on fifty miles of the coast of the Pacific Ocean. There he built luxurious mansions and displayed the art he collected from all over the world. Julia went there three weekends a month to help design the buildings William wanted. She did so for more than twenty years, along with operating her own architectural firm during the week.

Julia designed more than seven hundred buildings in her professional career. These included schools, churches, hospitals, YWCAs, community centers, apartments, hotels, and family residences. Her buildings are a testament to the excellent contributions women have made to architecture.

1. Julia made three attempts at passing an entrance exam to her French college before she passed it. What does that tell you about her?
2. Julia spent much of her time drawing and planning buildings. Draw a picture of your favorite building, or design one using pattern blocks or geometric solids. What will the building be used for?
3. If Julia Morgan came to visit you, what interesting architectural structure would you take her to see in your community? Why?

SOCIAL STUDIES

1. Find books in the library that have photographs of Julia's architecture. What do you like and dislike about her style?
2. Look at the architecture of Frank Lloyd Wright in a reference or architecture book. In your opinion, how do his designs differ from Julia's?
3. Hearst Castle, with its Roman temple, private theater, and huge swimming pools, is on the former Hearst estate in San Simeon, California. Locate San Simeon on a map. See if you can find a book on the Hearst Castle in the library. Look through the pictures and choose your favorite thing about the estate.
4. What direction is San Francisco from San Simeon? From your home, how many states would you have to travel through to get to San Francisco?

FURTHER READING

Gibbons, Gail. *Up Goes the Skyscraper*. American Women of Achievement Series. New York: Four Winds Press, 1986.

James, Cary. *Julia Morgan*. New York: Chelsea House Publishers, 1990.

Kett-O'Connor, Pamela. *Julia Morgan*. Vero Beach, FL: Rourke Publications, 1993.

Macaulay, David. *Castle*. Boston: Houghton Mifflin, 1982.

Wadsworth, Ginger. *Julia Morgan: Architect of Dreams*. Minneapolis, MN: Lerner Group, 1990.

Wilkinson, Philip. *Building*. Eyewitness Books. New York: Alfred A. Knopf, 1995.

GRANDMA MOSES (Anna Mary Robertson) ★ 1860–1961

Folk Artist

Anna Mary Robertson was born on a farm in Washington County in the state of New York. As a child Anna Mary enjoyed the colors she found around her. Her art materials were flour paste, slack lime, ground ocher, twigs, grass, bark, and sawdust. She would paint on broken dishes, old crocks, and jugs.

Anna Mary helped to earn money for her family. At twelve years of age, she went to work for a fairly wealthy man and his wife, the Whitesides, at three dollars a month.

But Anna Mary received more than pay. The Whitesides had lithographic prints on the walls made by two famous men named Currier and Ives. Mr. Whiteside saw how interested Anna Mary was in drawing and painting, so he gave her a box of wax crayons and chalk crayons.

Anna Mary then worked for a number of families. She had the reputation of being the best working girl in the county. While she was still in her twenties, she worked for a family that had a hired man named Thomas Salmon Moses. They fell in love, married, and moved south to the state of Virginia.

After nineteen years, Thomas and Anna Mary decided to move back to Eagle Bridge in Washington County, New York. They had saved enough money to buy a farm of their own and still have some cash left over. Thomas died at seventy-seven years of age. Anna Mary was sixty-seven. Because rheumatism stiffened her fingers, she found it hard to sew and embroider. So when she turned seventy, someone suggested that she paint pictures, which was easier for her to do. Anna Mary liked the idea and thought this would be a good time for people to start calling her "Grandma."

In the 1930s she started entering her pictures at the county fair, along with her jams and jellies. Louis Caldor, an art dealer from New York City, happened to see four of her paintings in the window of the local drug store. He was impressed and bought all of them. He wanted to meet the artist, but she was not at home. Grandma's daughter-in-law told Mr. Caldor that she thought Grandma had ten more paintings around. He said he would come by the next day and buy them.

Grandma Moses could hardly sleep that night because she only had eight paintings. Then she remembered that she had brought a large one from Virginia. She cut it in half and made two pictures. Now she had ten, and Mr. Caldor bought them all.

Dr. Otto Kallir became her representative and organized a company called Grandma Moses Properties, Inc. When she received a check for several thousand dollars from him, Grandma passed it out to her family and friends.

Grandma Moses wrote her biography and continued to paint pictures through her eighties and nineties. She finished more than a thousand of them. Grandma became friends with United States presidents and even danced with her doctor on her hundredth birthday. He was only eighty-four. She died at the age of 101 years, 3 months, and 6 days.

1. What did you find most extraordinary about Grandma Moses?

2. It is 1960 and you are a newspaper reporter. Write a newspaper article about Grandma Moses on her 100th birthday. Describe her life, her achievements, and her attitude.

3. What three relatives do you think would most enjoy this biography? Why?

4. Prepare to read Grandma Moses's biography to younger children or to people at a nursing home. Read from some of the books in the Further Reading section that follows to gain more information about Grandma Moses so you can better answer questions about her.

SOCIAL STUDIES

1. In a reference or art book, look at pictures painted by Grandma Moses. What do you like and dislike about her style of painting? Pretend you are an art critic and share your views with the class.

2. Read about Currier and Ives in a reference or art book. Choose one picture and display it for the class. Explain why you like it.

3. Choose one painting by Grandma Moses and try to copy it in your own way. How is your style different from hers?

4. If Grandma Moses were asked to advertise products now, what would she advertise?

FURTHER READING

Laing, Martha. *Grandma Moses: The Grand Old Lady of American Art*. Charlotteville, NY: SamHar Press, 1972.

Moore, Clement C. *The Grandma Moses Night Before Christmas*. New York: Random House, 1991.

Abolitionist, Minister, Women's Rights Leader

In the late 1700s, as a little girl, Lucretia lived on an island called Nantucket, thirty miles off the coast of Massachusetts. The winters were bitterly cold, with icy winds blowing across the waters of the Atlantic Ocean. Lucretia's brother and sisters missed their father, for he was the master on a whaling ship and was gone for long periods of time. The last trip stretched into three years and there was no word from him.

Whenever a ship sailed into port, the town crier called out its arrival to the community. Often Lucretia climbed the stairs to the roof and looked out from the "widow's walk" for a glimpse of a ship on the horizon. When she saw a ship heading for their port, she prayed it carried her father. Lucretia was seven years old when he had left the last time. Now she was ten.

Her father finally came home. He told of his capture off the Pacific coast of South America and his arrest for hunting seals in Spanish waters. Then he was released to go wherever he wanted by the best way he could. He decided that home with his family was the greatest place for him. Lucretia was delighted.

When Lucretia was twenty-eight, she became a Quaker minister. She believed that slavery was wrong and, as an abolitionist and Quaker minister, she spoke out against it.

Lucretia was different from the radical abolitionists of that time. Although she was a very determined woman, she was gentle and kind when dealing with people. Lucretia and James taught black children in a special school and used their home as part of the Underground Railroad to help slaves reach Canada and freedom.

Lucretia helped to form antislavery groups and became the enemy of many who favored slavery. One night, a group of rowdy men burned a hall where abolitionists met and spoke. Then the men decided to find where Lucretia and James, her husband, lived and burn down their house. Before the crowd got there, however, James and Lucretia were warned. James took their children to a neighbor for safety. Then he and Lucretia waited in the front room for the ruffians to come. But a young friend of theirs guided the gang down the wrong street, and they could not find the house.

In 1840 Lucretia was one of four women delegates to go to an antislavery meeting in England. She was excited, for the British had outlawed slavery in their country. James went with her. When they got to the meeting, she met Elizabeth Cady Stanton, another abolitionist. Yet the women were not allowed to participate. Lucretia came home more than an abolitionist: she was determined to gain equal rights for women too.

When Abraham Lincoln signed the Emancipation Proclamation freeing the slaves, part of Lucretia's mission in life was fulfilled. She continued to work for equality for all. Even though Lucretia Mott did not live to see the day when the law of the land treated men and women equally, her work and her commitment helped to make it possible.

People of Purpose

1. Try to imagine what young Lucretia Mott felt when waiting three years for her father to return. Pretend you are waiting in the observation tower at Cape Canaveral, Florida, for a parent coming home from a long space voyage. What thoughts are going through your mind? Write them down.

2. Look up the term *widow's walk* in a dictionary. Why do you think it is called a *widow's walk*?

3. What other alternatives, besides waiting quietly, did Lucretia and James have when they knew a gang was coming to burn their house? Why do you think they just waited quietly?

4. What was unfair about the fact that women could not participate in the antislavery meeting in England? Write a letter to Lucretia telling her your feelings about it.

SOCIAL STUDIES

1. Read about the Quaker faith in a reference book. What do you like and dislike about what you learned?

2. If Lucretia Mott were alive today, what do you think she would be doing? What social issues would she be devoted to?

3. Read the first few sentences of the second paragraph of the Declaration of Independence. You will find the document in an encyclopedia. What do the sentences mean to you?

4. There are instances where children and adults in other countries are treated as prisoners and slaves and are forced to produce clothing and goods that are sold to United States consumers. Would you buy these products if you knew they were made by these workers? What if the clothes were less expensive than U.S.-made products? Debate these questions as a class.

FURTHER READING

Sawyer, Kem K. *Lucretia Mott: Friend of Justice*. Lowell, MA: Discovery Enterprises, Ltd., 1991.

Stein, R. Conrad. *The Bill of Rights*. Cornerstones of Freedom Series. Chicago: Childrens Press, 1992.

JOHN MUIR

★ 1838–1914

Explorer, Naturalist, Writer

John loved to run and run over the moors in Scotland. He was born in Dunbar, near Edinburgh. Dunbar Castle's thousand-year-old walls and rooms were great places for him and his friends to explore. Daniel, John's father, beat him when he left the yard at home, for he was afraid John would injure himself. Daniel Muir was a strict, religious man. He believed that whipping helped his son become good. But John continued to run because he loved the countryside, its plants and its animals.

One evening, John's father told his family they were moving to America. John was happy because he thought he would have more freedom there.

After dinner in the evenings, John's father read the Bible to the family, and the children went to bed at 8:00 P.M. John was told he could get up early in the morning if he wanted to read. So John got up at 1:00 A.M. and read for five hours by candlelight.

When he was twenty-two, John decided to leave home. He worked in a carriage factory, where a file pierced his right eye and his left eye went blind in sympathy. It was weeks before John could see again. He decided that in the future he would spend his time looking at nature. Soon after, he began a thousand-mile walk from Kentucky to Florida to observe plants and animals. He took three books with him: the New Testament, Milton's *Paradise Lost,* and Burns's *Poems.*

He went to New York City, but what he found there he called "terrible canyons." Then he read about the Yosemite Valley in California. John spent forty dollars for passage to the West Coast. To reach California, he sailed to the Isthmus of Panama, took a train across Panama to the Pacific Ocean side, and boarded another boat to San Francisco.

Yosemite's jagged mountains, sparkling lakes, and cascading waterfalls left John in awe. There John became concerned about the environment. Lumber companies were stripping the land of trees, and sheepherders let their sheep eat all the vegetation. He did not want to see millions of years of nature's work ruined.

John found a friend in President Theodore Roosevelt. The president camped out with John for four days and nights. John said he "stuffed him pretty well" with information about those who were damaging the environment. Finally, because of his influence, the United States Congress passed laws forming the national parks to protect special areas of natural beauty.

John married and had two daughters. He did well financially with a fruit farm, but his wife knew he was not happy as a farmer. She encouraged him to travel to Alaska and other wilderness areas when he was not needed on the farm. Later, he stopped farming altogether and wrote about the environment. His writing and speaking made him known as the Father of the National Parks.

1. How did John Muir's childhood prepare him for the career he eventually had?
2. What were the "terrible canyons" John Muir referred to when he went to New York City? Look at pictures of New York City in a reference book. Do the streets look like canyons to you? Would you rather visit New York City or a national park?
3. If you were to take a 1,000-mile walk, where would you go? What three books would you take with you?
4. Find some of John Muir's writings at the library. Choose a paragraph or sentence you like and copy it on a piece of paper. Then draw a picture to go along with the quotation. Explain to the class why you liked it.

SOCIAL STUDIES

1. Find Dunbar, Scotland, on a map. What sea borders it? What are the "moors"? Read about Scotland in a reference book and share what you find with your class.
2. On a map or globe, trace the route from New York City through Panama to San Francisco. Why do you think he chose this route instead of going straight west? Why did John not go by ship through the Panama Canal?
3. Look up Yosemite National Park in a reference or nature book. What interests you most about it? List five reasons why you think it is important to have national parks.
4. What happens to land stripped of trees and vegetation? Are there any areas near you that are barren? Write a brief protest against the stripping of land.

FURTHER READING

Anderson, Peter. *John Muir: Wilderness Prophet*. New York: Franklin Watts, 1996.

Douglas, William O. *Muir of the Mountains*. San Francisco: Sierra Club Books for Children, 1993.

Greene, Carol. *John Muir: Man of the Wild Places*. Rookie Biography Series. Chicago: Childrens Press, 1991.

Talmadge, Katherine S. *John Muir: At Home in the Wild*. Earthkeepers Series. New York: Twenty-First Century Books, 1993.

Tolan, Sally. *John Muir*. People Who Have Helped the World Series. Milwaukee, WI: Gareth Stevens Children's Books, 1989.

Wadsworth, Ginger. *John Muir: Wilderness Protector*. Minneapolis: Lerner Group, 1992.

MARGARET MURIE ★ 1902–

Environmentalist

The year was 1911. Margaret, nine years old, waited anxiously for the telegram from her stepfather that would tell the family to follow him to Fairbanks, Alaska. The federal government had appointed him to be the United States district attorney there. Finally, the telegram came and she and her mother prepared to leave Seattle, Washington, for their new home. Three days later, they boarded the steamer and headed north, where temperatures often dropped to twenty, thirty, and fifty degrees below zero.

When she was fifteen, Margaret's parents sent her back to Seattle to go to college because there were no schools of higher education in Alaska at that time. After changing from one dogsled to another, she boarded a steamer bound for the United States. When she returned for a visit two years later, she traveled by car on a newly completed road.

In Alaska she met Olaus, a field biologist for the United States government. Olaus was studying Alaska's great caribou herds. Margaret decided to stay in Alaska because the University of Alaska in Fairbanks was now open for classes and, of course, there was Olaus. Margaret was the only senior at the University of Alaska. She became the first, and only person that year, to graduate from the new school. She and Olaus were married on her twenty-second birthday.

Margaret learned from Olaus how a scientist works. She kept accurate records for him of small creatures, such as the mouse, and large creatures, such as the caribou. There were

times when Olaus had to leave Margaret alone at their base camp so he could go out and collect specimens. Margaret worried that he might not come back and wondered what she would do with no one around. But as wild as Alaska was, she loved this country "on top of the world."

Now there were four children in the family. Margaret and Olaus took them on their trips into the quiet wilderness. The children were delighted and kept themselves busy from morning until night.

Olaus left government work so that he and Margaret could spend their time telling the people what was happening to the American wilderness. For years, Margaret and Olaus traveled and spoke to anyone who would listen. They joined with other groups to stop the building of dams that flooded large wilderness refuge areas. They urged the creation of wildlife sanctuaries for migrating birds. Margaret kept a diary during these years and it became her first book.

When Olaus died of cancer in 1963, Margaret thought she could not go on, but she did. As a National Park Service consultant she continued to speak for the environment. In the summer of 1964, she was invited to the White House by President Lyndon B. Johnson. There he signed the Wilderness Act, which placed nine million acres of forestland in national forests under the protection of the U.S. government. Margaret had done her part.

1. List ten things you learned about Margaret Murie. Compare your list with a partner's.
2. Pretend you are Margaret waiting for Olaus at your base camp deep in the wilds of Alaska. If he does not return, what will you do? Write what you are thinking.
3. Margaret called Alaska the country "on top of the world." What do you think she meant by that?
4. Write four reasons why you would or would not like to have a life like Margaret's.

SOCIAL STUDIES

1. Read about Alaska in a reference book. When did it become a state? Share with the class what you find most interesting about Alaska.
2. On a map or globe, trace the route from Fairbanks to Anchorage, Alaska, and on to Seattle, Washington. Do you know anyone, perhaps a family member, who had to travel farther to college than Margaret? How far?
3. Make a list of ten necessary things you would need on a dogsled trip into the Alaskan wilds. Compare your list with those of your classmates. What one or two things could you possibly eliminate?
4. What is the greatest danger to the survival of wild species of animals?

FURTHER READING

Bryant, Jennifer. *Margaret Murie: A Wilderness Life*. Earthkeepers Series. New York: Twenty-First Century Books, 1993.

Heinrichs, Ann. *Alaska*. America the Beautiful Series. Chicago: Childrens Press, 1991.

Markham, Adam. *The Environment*. World Issues Series. Vero Beach, FL: Rourke Enterprises, Inc., 1988.

Stefoff, Rebecca. *Environmental Movement*. Social Reform Movements Series. New York: Facts on Files, Inc., 1995.

FLORENCE NIGHTINGALE 1820–1910

Founder of the Nursing Profession

In 1837 Florence wrote on her February diary page these words: "God spoke to me and called me to His service." Florence kept this call to herself throughout her young life in England. Later, she found out what that service was.

Florence's father, William Nightingale, inherited a great amount of wealth. When he married Fanny, they took a long honeymoon throughout Europe. During their time in Europe, two girls were born. They were in Florence, Italy, when Florence was born.

When older, Florence talked to her parents and sister about working in a hospital. They were appalled. They thought only women who were drunkards and unable to do other work served in hospitals.

Florence visited and then studied at a very clean hospital in Germany called Kaiserwerth, where the nurses received excellent training. Florence studied reports and surveys about health matters and became quite knowledgeable.

When she returned to England at age thirty-two, she was considered an expert and was put in charge of the Institution for Sick Gentlewomen in Distressed Circumstances. She made sure the women patients had good food, clean sheets, and were warm. She even provided flowers to brighten up the rooms.

The British, French, and Turkish governments went to war against Russia in 1854. The fighting was fierce on the Crimean peninsula around Sevastapol and Balaklava. Soldiers received very poor care. More were dying from diseases, such as cholera, than from injuries received on the battlefield. Florence went with

thirty-eight hand-picked nurses to a British hospital in Turkey. The conditions there were beyond description. There were no supplies; operations were performed on the soldiers on their beds; and the newly wounded had to be placed in the corridors and stairwells. Not only that, the army doctors did not even want the nurses there.

Florence and her nurses took money she had collected and bought clean bedding and clothes for the soldiers. She hired workers in the area to clean the toilet drains that had backed up. When a dead horse was found to be contaminating the water supply, she had it removed. She and her nurses put up screens around beds where operations were taking place, and men with infectious diseases were put in rooms away from the other soldiers. The death rate in the hospital soon fell by two-thirds.

Florence spent many nights going through the hospital, comforting the wounded and dying. She wrote hundreds of letters for them. She became known as the "Lady with the Lamp" because of her nightly walks.

Soon the world knew about Florence Nightingale. She began a training school for nurses and created a uniform with a white hat and apron.

Her years of hard work, plus illness, put Florence in bed the last ten years of her life. Even then, she spent her time writing about ways the nursing profession could relieve suffering.

1. Read again what Florence Nightingale wrote in her diary in February 1837. What did her "call" turn out to be? What would be the most noble call of service that you could receive? Why?
2. Write an obituary for Florence Nightingale. Give it an interesting title.
3. With a partner, compose a poem about Florence's visiting wounded soldiers and writing letters for them during the night hours.
4. Write a paragraph on why you would or would not want to be a nurse.

SOCIAL STUDIES

1. Find the Crimean peninsula on a map. (It is now part of Ukraine. Sevastopol and Balaklava are on its southern tip.) What direction from the Crimean peninsula is Turkey?
2. Turkey is separated from the Crimean Peninsula by what body of water?
3. What do you think would be the most exciting medical advance that Florence would find if she came back to this present day?

FURTHER READING

Adler, David A. *A Picture Book of Florence Nightingale*. New York: Holiday House, 1992.

Bull, Angela. *Florence Nightingale*. Profiles Series. London: Trafalgar, 1991.

Shore, Donna. *Florence Nightingale*. What Made Them Great Series. Englewood Cliffs, NJ: Silver Burdett Press, 1990.

ALFRED NOBEL ★ 1833–1896

Industrialist, Inventor, Founder of the Nobel Prizes

Alfred Nobel of Sweden spent much of his early life in bed. He often had headaches, colds, poor digestion, and back problems. His mother taught him at home. During a brief period, when he was able to go to school, he did quite well. He read widely, drew, and tried to understand how things worked. He was much like his inventor father, Immanuel, who tested and designed torpedoes and mines that exploded in the sea.

In a few years, Immanuel Nobel decided that his boys had had enough school and should go to work. By then the Nobels were quite prosperous, so Robert and Ludwig went to work for their father. Alfred, who at sixteen was already an industrial chemist, was sent on a two-year tour of many countries to make contacts for his father's business. He became very interested in explosives and spent time in many laboratories talking to scientists. He also took time to write poems and plays and become proficient in several languages.

Emil was the only one of the boys to graduate from college. Alfred asked Emil to help him package nitroglycerin so it would be safer to use. But tragedy struck. Emil and an assistant were filling a large order of explosives for blasting a railroad tunnel when the explosives accidentally blew up. Emil and the assistant were killed. Alfred was away on business at the time. No one knew for sure how the accident had happened.

Alfred learned to mix *kieselguhr*, a porous kind of earth, with nitroglycerin. The earth soaked up the oily nitroglycerin and the result-ing explosive became like putty. It was easy to transport, safe, and reliable. Alfred called it "dynamite," from the Greek word *dunamis*, meaning power or force. Dynamite would not explode if it were placed in fire or hurled at a wall. What it needed to explode was a blasting cap. Alfred invented one.

Many uses were found for dynamite. People carved tunnels through mountains, quarried marble for buildings, mined coal, and built dams with it. Engineers used it to build the Panama Canal. The sculptor Gutzon Borglum used it to blast out the figures of the U.S. presidents on Mount Rushmore. The New York subway system and the Erie Barge Canal were made more cheaply and quickly because of dynamite.

Dynamite was not only used for peaceful purposes. Military men used it to destroy each other's armies. This bothered Alfred greatly. When his brother Ludwig died, a newspaper confused the two brothers and wrote that Alfred, "the merchant of death," was dead.

Alfred vowed to clear the Nobel name. In his will, he left all his money—at the time about nine million dollars—for prizes. That money has continued to earn interest, and the interest pays for the prizes. Every year, the prize money is divided among people around the world for their work of importance to humanity.

Alfred's yearly prizes have encouraged people to use their talents for the benefit of humanity. The profits on explosives now reward men and women of purpose around the world.

1. Share with a partner the things you most admired about Alfred Nobel.
2. What kind of confidence did Immanuel Nobel have in his son Alfred by sending him at sixteen on a tour of European countries to make contacts for his business? What does that tell you about Alfred?
3. Fold a sheet of paper in half the long way. On the left side, write five facts about Alfred Nobel. On the right side, write your thoughts or feelings in response to these facts.
4. What does the phrase "the merchant of death" mean to you?

SOCIAL STUDIES

1. Read about dynamite and its uses in a reference book. Can you think of another invention that can be used for both good and bad purposes?
2. Read about the Nobel Prizes in a reference work or textbook. How many are awarded each year? What areas do they honor?
3. If you had a great deal of money to leave to charities upon your death, what kinds of charities would you leave it to? Why?

FURTHER READING

Aaseng, Nathan. *The Peace Seekers: The Nobel Peace Prize*. Minneapolis, MN: Lerner Publications Company, 1987.

SANDRA DAY O'CONNOR ★ 1930–

Supreme Court Justice

Sandra loved the 170,000-acre ranch in Arizona. In the summers she rode bareback on the horses, fished with a line made out of string and a safety-pin hook, and shot "varmints" for her dad with her .22 rifle.

Many years before, her grandfather, Henry Day, went to Mexico. He bought six thousand head of cattle in Mexico and brought them back to the Lazy B Ranch. Her father, Harry Day, inherited that ranch. He married Ada Mae Wilke in 1928. Sandra's father taught her riding, roping, and shooting. Her mother, a college graduate, was more interested in academics and culture. The combination gave Sandra a well-rounded view of life.

Sandra applied for entrance to Stanford University, located about thirty miles south of San Francisco, California, and was accepted. While at Stanford, she was named an editor of the *Stanford Law Review,* which was a high honor. Sandra spent many hours in the library editing manuscripts and checking them for facts. While in the library, she met another law student, John Jay O'Connor III, who was doing the same type of work. Two years later they were married at the Lazy B Ranch.

Sandra graduated third in her class and took a job as a deputy county attorney in California. John graduated the following year. Afterward, they returned to Arizona, and John entered law practice with a firm.

Sandra and John had three sons. While raising her family, Sandra stayed busy volunteering at the YMCA, the Phoenix Historical Society, and as a juvenile court referee. Then she campaigned for the position of trial judge in Phoenix and won. There she heard divorce cases and drug cases and presided over murder trials.

Her next move came with an appointment to the Arizona Court of Appeals. Now her cases were not about guilt or innocence. They were about interpretations of the law and opinions about whether evidence in a previous trial was gathered legally or illegally. Along with two other judges, she wrote these opinions. Sandra also gave more and more public speeches on a wide range of issues.

In 1981 President Reagan called her to the White House. One of the Supreme Court justices had retired, and Sandra's name was proposed as his replacement as an associate justice of the Court. President Reagan found her delightful and an excellent choice. The committee voted 17 to 0 to confirm her appointment, and the full Senate approved her 99 to 0. It was the first time in United States history that a woman would be able to make decisions at the highest court in the land.

Sandra Day O'Connor became the first woman Supreme Court justice. She thought that Abigail Adams, the wife of the second president of the United States, would be pleased to know that.

Sandra sometimes votes with the majority, which is five of the nine justices, and sometimes she does not. But she votes each time on the merits of how she views a specific case. Her decisions are those of a judge, who happens to be a woman.

1. How would you describe Sandra Day O'Connor to a friend who had never heard of her?
2. Make two drawings, one of Sandra riding a horse and the other of her in her Supreme Court robe. Write an appropriate caption under each.
3. Why did Sandra think Abigail Adams would be pleased with her appointment to the Supreme Court?
4. What did you learn about Sandra's life that could influence your life?

SOCIAL STUDIES

1. On a map, find the following places where Sandra lived: Stanford University (in Palo Alto, California); Germany; Phoenix, Arizona; and Washington, D.C. Which ones seem like the most interesting places to visit? Why?
2. Read about the U.S. Supreme Court in a reference book. What purpose does it serve? How many justices are there? How are they appointed?
3. Read the last sentence of Sandra's biography. What does it mean? If you were a Supreme Court justice, could you make decisions without regard to your being a woman or a man?
4. Who among your classmates do you think will rise, like Sandra, to a position of honor? Why? Keep your answer in a safe place and look at it forty years from now. Perhaps you can read it at a high school reunion.

FURTHER READING

Herda, D. J. *Sandra Day O'Connor: Independent Thinker.* Justices of the Supreme Court. Springfield, NJ: Enslow Publishers, 1995.

Kronenwetter, Michael. *The Supreme Court of the United States.* American Government in Action Series. Springfield, NJ: Enslow Publishers, 1996.

ROSA LEE PARKS ★ 1913–

Civil Rights Activist

In the early part of the twentieth century, there were white men in Pine Level, Alabama, who intensely disliked African Americans. Some of them wrapped themselves in white sheets and put on white pointed hoods to cover their faces. They rode around the countryside at night and frightened African Americans so they would not register to vote. They burned crosses in people's yards, burned churches, and hurt and killed people. They called themselves the Ku Klux Klan. They hated not only African Americans; they also hated Jews, Roman Catholics, and foreigners. Often Rosa could not sleep for fear they would come to her grandparents' farm.

When African Americans rode the buses in Montgomery, Alabama, they had to sit in the back. First, they went in the front door and paid their fare. Then they had to go out the front door and enter the back door to get on the bus. Sometimes, a bus driver would leave before they reached the back door. This happened to Rosa.

One day in 1955, Rosa was coming home from work in downtown Montgomery. She got on the Cleveland Avenue bus and sat in the first row of the section for African American passengers. The bus filled up and a white man had no place to sit. The bus driver told Rosa and three African American men to move back because he was extending the white section one more row for the white man to have a seat. African Americans were not allowed to sit in the same row as white people. Rosa refused and was arrested, put in jail, and had to have a lawyer get her out on a one-hundred-dollar bond. She was found guilty and her fine came to ten dollars, plus an extra four dollars for processing the arrest.

In reaction to her treatment, the Women's Political Council passed out fifty-two thousand leaflets urging African Americans to refuse to use the buses until all people could sit where they pleased. Ministers such as Martin Luther King, Jr., and Ralph Abernathy and their congregations became involved.

Rosa was advised not to pay the fine so her case could proceed through the courts. It went from one court to another until it got to the U.S. Supreme Court in Washington, D.C. This procedure took a year. During that time, the African American citizens of Montgomery boycotted the bus company. African American churches and other organizations helped people get to work in cars. Some rode horse-drawn wagons and, in one case, a mule. But many African Americans walked to work that year. On December 20, 1956, the Supreme Court upheld a lower court order that the Montgomery buses must be integrated.

Because of her bravery, Rosa received many honors: the Martin Luther King, Jr., Nonviolent Award, the Eleanor Roosevelt Woman of Courage Award, and the Presidential Medal of Freedom. She became known as "the mother of the civil rights movement." And Cleveland Avenue in Montgomery was renamed Rosa Parks Boulevard.

1. Write three newspaper headlines that would be appropriate to use as titles for Rosa Parks's biography. Compare your headlines with a classmate's.

2. With a small group, write a rap song describing Rosa Parks's life or some phase of it—perhaps the bus episode. Perform it for the class.

3. Pantomime, without words, Rosa's removal from the Montgomery bus. You will need students for Rosa, the bus driver, and a policeman. After the presentation, discuss your feelings.

4. Try to think of an experience where you were dealt with unfairly. What could you do if it happened again?

SOCIAL STUDIES

1. Read about the Ku Klux Klan in a reference book. Write a report on what you learned and share it with the class.

2. Pretend Rosa came to visit you. To what places could both of you now go together, places you could not have gone in the past? Draw a picture of Rosa and you at one of these places.

3. Discuss with a small group the gains you think minorities have made in the last fifty years. What still needs to be accomplished? Make a list and compare it with other groups' lists.

4. How well do you think people of various races will tolerate each other by the year 2050? Will the problems be better, worse, or the same? Why?

FURTHER READING

Adler, David A. *A Picture Book of Rosa Parks*. Picture Book Biography Series. New York: Holiday House, 1993.

Altman, Susan. *Extraordinary Black Americans from Colonial to Contemporary Times*. Chicago: Childrens Press, 1989.

Celsi, Teresa. *Rosa Parks and the Montgomery Bus Boycott*. Gateway Civil Rights Series. Brookfield, CT: The Millbrook Press, 1991.

Friese, Kai. *Rosa Parks: The Movement Organizes*. Englewood Cliffs, NJ: Silver Burdett Press, 1990.

Greenfield, Eloise. *Rosa Parks*. New York: HarperCollins, 1995.

Parks, Rosa. *Rosa Parks*. New York: HarperCollins Children's Books, 1996.

Turner, Glennette Tilley. *Take a Walk in Their Shoes*. New York: Puffin Books, 1992.

LOUIS PASTEUR ★ 1822–1895

Scientist

Eight-year-old Louis Pasteur listened in horror as several people in the village of Arbois, France, screamed in pain. They were being cauterized for the wolf bites they had suffered. At that time, this was the treatment for rabies. The person was branded with a hot iron on the flesh where the bites punctured the skin. Even with this treatment, however, few people lived.

Louis studied chemistry at the École Normale in Paris. When he was twenty-six, his study of crystals brought him instant fame. Louis founded *stereochemistry*, the study of the arrangement of atoms in chemical substances. This resulted in his appointment to the University of Strasbourg as a chemistry teacher.

In Strasbourg he met Marie Laurent and they were married. Marie took notes for him and cared for him as he worked in his laboratory.

A businessman asked Louis for help. The man's company made vinegar from beet juice. Sometimes the process of fermentation failed, and he would lose a lot of money. Louis looked at the juice through his microscope and found the problem: microorganisms—very small organisms seen only under a microscope. He heated the juice to 140°F (60°C), and the unwanted microorganisms died. He used the same process for wine, beer, and milk. The procedure became known as pasteurization in his honor.

Anthrax was another problem on which Louis worked. This infectious disease attacked sheep and cattle. Sometimes humans caught it, and it usually resulted in death. Louis inoculated sheep with weakened anthrax germs (a vaccine) so the sheep would get a low-grade disease and develop immunity to it. This way they resisted the disease when contacting the strong anthrax germs. The process was called *inoculation*.

In 1885 Pasteur and his associates tried to find a cure for rabies. When a mad dog bit a person, the saliva, with its germs, entered the victim's bloodstream. Animal experiments were successful, but experiments on humans were yet to be tried.

One day, Joseph Meister's mother brought her little boy to Louis. Joseph had fourteen rabid-dog bites. "Help my son!" she cried. Louis was not sure. If the boy had no infection, Louis's inoculation could give the boy the disease. But Louis could not wait. He gave Joseph the anti-rabies injections and the boy lived.

Soon after, nineteen peasants from Russia came to Louis. A rabid wolf had bitten all of them two weeks before. Louis's inoculations saved sixteen of them.

Many years after Louis Pasteur died, Joseph Meister was the gatekeeper at the tomb in Paris where Louis lay buried. World War II was in progress. The Germans had invaded Paris. A Nazi officer wanted to view Louis's crypt. Joseph Meister committed suicide rather than let an enemy take even one glimpse of his beloved Louis Pasteur's tomb.

Louis Pasteur's genius now provides us safe milk and lifetime freedom from many diseases.

1. Why do you think Louis Pasteur was greatly loved?
2. Fill in this sentence: I enjoyed the biography of Louis Pasteur because _____.
3. Louis Pasteur once said, "A man of science should think of what will be said of him in the following century, not of the insults or compliments of one day." Explain what this statement means. How does it apply to Louis? Then list three things you would want people to say about you fifty years from now.
4. With two partners, make up bumper stickers about Louis Pasteur. Share them with the class.

SOCIAL STUDIES

1. With a partner, read about inoculations in a reference book. Discuss how they work. What diseases have you been inoculated against?
2. Louis Pasteur wrote, "[T]he future will belong not to the conquerors but to the saviors of mankind." Explain what he meant. Then list three conquerors and three saviors you know about who fit Louis's quote.
3. Read more about Louis Pasteur. List some of his accomplishments. Number your list, putting those of greatest benefit to society first. See how your list compares with your classmates'.
4. Fill in this sentence: The disease that I think needs conquering most is

   _____

   because_____
   _____
   _____.

   Share and compare answers with a small group.

FURTHER READING

Curtis, Robert H. *Medicine*. Great Lives Series. New York: Simon & Schuster Children's Books, 1993.

Greene, Carol. *Louis Pasteur: Enemy of Disease*. Rookie Biography Series. Chicago: Childrens Press, 1990.

Newfield, Marcia. *The Life of Louis Pasteur*. Pioneers in Health and Medicine Series. Frederick, MD: Twenty-First Century Books, 1991.

Parker, Steve. *Louis Pasteur and Germs*. Science Discoveries Series. New York: Chelsea House Publishers, 1995.

Sabin, Francene. *Louis Pasteur: Young Scientist*. Mahwah, NJ: Troll Communications, 1983.

FRANCES PERKINS 1880–1965

Secretary of Labor

Fannie Perkins loved playing hide-and-seek on her family's farm in New England. One day, she dashed in and out of the barn and accidentally tumbled out of the loft, landing on her back. Her back hurt for a long time, but the pain finally stopped.

Many years later, President Franklin Roosevelt appointed her to his cabinet. Before taking office, she had to have a routine medical examination. It was then that the doctors discovered that she had broken her back many years before!

In 1911 a tragic accident at the Triangle Shirtwaist Company made a profound impression on Frances. The workers, mostly young girls and women, had gone on strike the previous year. The tall building in which they worked had no working fire escapes, and the doors in the building were kept locked. The employees decided to strike for safer working conditions. But the owners refused to listen. They warned the strikers that they would hire other people to take their places if they did not return to work. Not wanting to lose their jobs, they all returned to work.

The following year, disaster struck. A fire trapped the workers on the upper floors of the factory. The fire department had no ladders tall enough to get them out, so many fell to their deaths. In all, 146 women and girls perished in the fire.

Frances was having tea with friends nearby when she heard the fire engines. She ran to the scene and saw the women falling but could do nothing to help them.

Frances became an outspoken critic of such abuse. She worked for the state of New York and lobbied for a shorter work week so laborers would not tire and accidentally hurt themselves at their machines. She toiled to limit child labor and the hours women and boys under eighteen worked. Largely because of her efforts, a forty-eight-hour work week replaced the fifty-four-hour work week in the state of New York. Frances also helped pass legislation for improved sanitary conditions, safety in factories, and compensation for workers who were injured on their jobs.

When President Franklin Roosevelt appointed Frances as secretary of the Department of Labor in 1933, she became the first woman to serve in the United States Cabinet.

In the next few years, Frances was responsible for much of the New Deal legislation that helped the country out of the Great Depression of the 1930s. She was also responsible for directing the Social Security Act, which now affects practically every U.S. worker.

Frances spent twelve years as secretary of labor and resigned after President Roosevelt died in office. In 1946 President Truman appointed her a member of the United States Civil Service Commission, where she served until 1953.

Frances passed away at eighty-five. Before her death she said, "You just can't be afraid . . . if you're going to accomplish anything."

READING

1. Frances Perkins said, "You just can't be afraid . . . if you're going to accomplish anything." How does this apply to her life? What does this quote mean to you?

2. Without referring to the biography, what five things do you remember about Frances Perkins?

3. Why does it often take a tragic accident, such as the Triangle Shirtwaist Company fire, to get passed a law that could have prevented it? What can we learn from this incident?

SOCIAL STUDIES

1. What is the president's cabinet? Who makes up the cabinet? How do they become members? See if you can find out why it is called the "cabinet." How many women are presently in the cabinet?

2. At what age can children in your state begin part-time work? How many hours are they permitted to work?

3. What does the secretary of labor do? Who is the current secretary of labor? Write him or her a letter concerning something you would like improved about your parents' or family members' working conditions. Your parents or family members can give you ideas.

FURTHER READING

Colman, Penny. *A Woman Unafraid: The Achievements of Frances Perkins*. New York: Antheneum, 1993.

Summer, Lila, and Samuel B. Woods. *The Judiciary: Laws We Live By*. Good Citizenship Library. Austin, TX: Raintree Steck-Vaughn Company, 1992.

BEATRIX POTTER ★ 1866–1943

Author and Illustrator

In London, England, young Beatrix lived a very lonely life. Her parents were wealthy, and at that time children, especially daughters of well-to-do English parents, were taught at home by governesses. Beatrix spent her days drawing plants and animals and had the companionship of her brother Bertram, who was five years younger than she. Beatrix kept a daily journal of her life and at fifteen began writing it in code so no one would know her secret thoughts.

During summers the family rented a home in Scotland. Beatrix enjoyed her time in the country and spent it drawing the cottages, gardens, and animals.

When Beatrix turned nineteen, she was provided with a teacher named Annie, who was just three years older than she. Annie was hired for the purposes of providing companionship and teaching languages. Now Beatrix had a friend. Two years later, Annie married, but her friendship with Annie changed the course of Beatrix's life a few years later.

Annie had a little boy named Noel, who became ill. To cheer him up, Beatrix wrote Noel a letter in the form of a story about four rabbits: Flopsy, Mopsy, Cotton-tail, and Peter. She asked Annie to return the letter that she had written to Noel and then rewrote it as a small book for children: *The Tale of Peter Rabbit*. No publisher was interested, however. Taking her savings from the bank, Beatrix had 250 copies printed and proceeded to take them to a bookstore. The owner displayed the books for her and they sold.

A publisher saw the book and told Beatrix he would print it for her. At thirty-six she began to earn money with her writing. In 1905 she used her earnings to buy Hill Top Farm in the Lake District in northern England.

An editor named Norman Warne encouraged her to write more books. He also asked her to marry him. They were in love, but Beatrix's parents objected because they saw him as merely a common worker. Unfortunately, Norman died of leukemia before they could marry.

In 1909 Beatrix bought Castle Cottage next to Hill Top Farm. A lawyer, William Heelis, helped her make the arrangements. They were attracted to each other. Even though her parents disapproved, she went ahead and married him. Beatrix was now forty-nine years old.

Beatrix continued to write stories and illustrate them. Her animal books sold in many different languages all over the world. She continued to buy more farmland and turned the farms into museums where tourists could see how life used to be.

Beatrix remained a very private and modest person throughout her life. After her death at seventy-seven, the secret code she had developed for her private journals was deciphered. She left four-thousand acres of farms, pastures, and woods to the National Trust, an organization that protects old buildings and lands in England. Her *Tales* books numbered twenty-three. They were considered the first modern picture books.

1. Read or reread one of the tales written and illustrated by Beatrix Potter. Summarize the story for the class. Compare it to the summaries of your classmates. What do Beatrix's tales have in common? Why do you think her tales are still so popular?

2. Pretend Beatrix just entered your classroom. What questions would you ask her?

3. If Peter Rabbit wrote you for advice about how to improve himself, what would you tell him? Share your answer with your classmates.

4. Write a story about your favorite animals and draw the illustrations.

SOCIAL STUDIES

1. Find London, northern England, and Scotland on a map or globe. Find some pictures of the English countryside in a travel book. How are they similar to the drawings of Beatrix Potter?

2. Compare the pictures of Sir John Everett Millais with those of Beatrix Potter. (They can be found in reference and art books.) How do they differ? Which do you prefer? Why?

3. A person's class, or status in life, was very important to Beatrix's parents. That is why they would not approve of the men who wanted to marry Beatrix. How do you feel about that?

4. Write a story about your favorite animals and draw the illustrations.

FURTHER READING

Collins, David R. *The Country Artist: A Story About Beatrix Potter.* Minneapolis: Carolrhoda Books, 1989.

Wallner, Alexandra. *Beatrix Potter.* New York: Holiday House, 1995.

COLIN LUTHER POWELL 1937–

Chairman of the Joint Chiefs of Staff, Statesman, Organizer

Colin was excited. Going to summer camp got him out of the hot city for the summer. Father Weeden of St. Margaret's Episcopal Church in the Bronx, New York City, had chosen him from all the boys in the parish to be their representative. But when he arrived, Colin stirred up trouble. He conspired with two other boys and together they left the camp, bought some beer, stole back in, and hid it in a toilet tank.

All the boys in the camp were called into a large meeting hall. The hidden beer had been discovered. The priest at the church camp did not threaten the assembled boys; he simply asked the person responsible for bringing beer to the campsite to stand up like a man and admit it. Colin could not sit still. He promptly stood up and admitted his guilt. Then the two other boys stood up too.

Immediately, Colin was sent home. His mother and father let him know how disappointed they were. As they talked to him, Father Weeden called to tell how Colin had stood on his feet and admitted his guilt, prompting the others to do likewise. His parents were pleased to learn how courageous he was to stand in front of everyone and admit he was wrong.

In public school Colin did average work. When he went to City College of New York, he joined the Reserve Officers Training Corps (ROTC) and entered their training program. Colin discovered that army life was the career he wanted. In his summer training at Fort Bragg, North Carolina, during his college years,

he was named "outstanding cadet." He graduated from CCNY with a degree in geology and entered the Army full time.

A few years later, on a blind date, he met Alma Vivian Johnson, a teacher of hearing-impaired children. They were married in August of 1962. Several months later Colin was sent to Vietnam to advise a South Vietnamese infantry battalion.

By April 1989 he commanded all the troops in the United States and was promoted in rank by President Bush. He became the first African American chairman of the Joint Chiefs of Staff. In this position he advised the president on matters of military policy. One of his first jobs was to settle a crisis in Panama. The dictator of that country was wanted on charges of drug trafficking.

As chairman, Colin's last big crisis was the Persian Gulf War. President Bush credited Colin Powell and the commander of the allied troops, General H. Norman Schwarzkopf, with bringing the battle with Iraq to a swift and successful conclusion. The war ended in forty-three days.

General Powell decided to retire from the Army. Since then, he has written his autobiography, given lectures, and spent more time with his family. Some people think he would make an excellent choice for president. Whatever he does, he will be honest with himself and with the country. Colin lists in his autobiography thirteen rules he follows. The fourteenth one is "It can be done!"

1. What does the incident at Colin's summer camp tell you about Colin Powell's character, even as a youth? Imagine yourself in the same position as Colin. Would you have admitted guilt in front of everyone? Why or why not?
2. Colin did average work in public school. When he got to college, he did much better. Think of some reasons why this could be so.
3. How would you describe Colin Powell to a friend who had never heard of him?
4. What does Colin's rule, "It can be done!" mean to you, personally? Write a paragraph about it.

SOCIAL STUDIES

1. Since he is retired from the Army, what do you think Colin Powell should do in the future? Write him a letter with your ideas.
2. Discuss with family members how they feel about the possibility of having Colin Powell as president of the United States. List some pros and cons for Colin Powell as a candidate. How would you vote if the election were today? Why?

FURTHER READING

Blue, Rose, and Corinne J. Naden. *Colin Powell: Straight to the Top*. Brookfield, CT: The Millbrook Press, 1991.

Landau, Elaine. *Colin Powell: Four-Star General*. New York: Franklin Watts, 1991.

JOSEPH PULITZER   ★ 1847–1911

Newspaper Publisher

As a young man in Mako, Hungary, Joseph learned to ride a horse well. He craved adventure and tried to enlist in three different European armies: the Austrian Army, Napoleon's Foreign Legion in France, and finally, the British Army. None would accept him because of his weak eyes and poor physique.

Undaunted, Joseph sailed for the United States because there was a need for soldiers in the Union Army during the Civil War. His riding experience enabled him to join the cavalry, but by then the war was nearly over.

Joseph was not able to find work in New York, so he sold his fine linen handkerchief for seventy-five cents. This money bought him food for a few days while he "rode the rods" on a train to St. Louis, Missouri. There he found work firing the boiler on a ferry, caring for mules, waiting tables in a restaurant, and digging graves because of a cholera epidemic that killed many people.

He heard about a job down river, working on a sugar plantation. Along with forty other men, Joseph paid an agent five dollars to take him down river. The agent left them stranded there. No jobs awaited the men, and they had to walk fifty miles back to St. Louis. A reporter asked Joseph to write about that experience, and his story was printed word-for-word in the German newspaper *Westliche Post*. Because of the story, Joseph got a job as a reporter.

Joseph learned English well and became a naturalized U.S. citizen. He saved his money and bought and sold newspaper companies for profit. He used the money he earned to study law and politics. He bought a German paper and resold it for a $20,000 profit. He purchased the *St. Louis Post* in 1872 for $3,000, and a few years later was able to buy the *St. Louis Dispatch* at a sheriff's sale for $2,700. Putting these two newspapers together, Joseph formed the *St. Louis Post-Dispatch*.

The *Post-Dispatch* became very profitable. He used it to speak out against lotteries, gambling, and those who avoided paying taxes. Joseph prodded the city to provide better streets.

When he was thirty-six, Joseph went back to New York. He sold the *Post-Dispatch* and used the money for a down payment on the *New York World*.

During the 1880s Joseph began to lose his sight. By 1889, he was blind and suffered from a nervous disorder that made him extremely sensitive to noise. Nevertheless, he maintained control of his publishing empire by hiring a team of secretaries to read to him from his newspaper. They also read to him from magazines, books, and competitors' newspapers. During those years he edited the *World* from his soundproof house or his yacht, where it was very quiet.

At his death Joseph Pulitzer left two million dollars to establish a graduate school of journalism at Columbia University. Part of his estate created the annual Pulitzer Prizes for achievement in journalism, literature, drama, and music.

134

1. Write an obituary for Joseph Pulitzer to appear in his newspaper. Give it a title.
2. What do you think are the two most important sentences in Joseph's biography? Why?
3. "Rode the rods" is a figure of speech meaning he stole a ride on a train. Some other figures of speech are "green with envy," "playing second fiddle," and "a ballpark figure." Do you know what these mean? What other figures of speech do you know?
4. Pretend you are a news anchorperson. Practice reading aloud from the biography of Joseph Pulitzer. Tape-record or videotape your reading and evaluate what parts you did well and what parts you could improve upon.

SOCIAL STUDIES

1. Find the country of Hungary on a map or globe. What countries touch its borders? Read about Hungary in a reference book and share three interesting facts with the class.
2. Look through the Pulitzer Prize winners lists in a reference book. Are there recent prizewinners from newspapers in your city or state?
3. Look through your local newspaper. Where would you find the opinions of the newspaper's publishers and editors? Write a letter to the editor stating your opinion on an issue that is important to you.
4. What should a newspaper do to (in Joseph Pulitzer's words) "battle for the people with earnest sincerity"? How does your local newspaper do this? If you were a journalist, how could you do so?

FURTHER READING

Gibbons, Gail. *Deadline! From News to Newspaper*. New York: HarperCollins Children's Books, 1987.

Granfield, Linda. *Extra! Extra! The Who, What, Where, When and Why of Newspapers*. New York: Orchard Books, 1994.

JEANNETTE RANKIN ★ 1880–1973

United States Congresswoman

NO MORE WAR

The sun gradually set over the mountains of Montana. Twelve-year-old Jeannette Rankin talked with her brother by the corral fence. They turned to watch their father walk Star, their horse, toward the barn. He shouted to her, "Get hot water, cloths, and the needle and thread!" Star's chest was bleeding from a barbed wire wound. Jeannette washed the wound and sutured it with the darning needle and thread.

Women received the right to vote in Montana in 1914 so Jeannette decided to run for the Congress of the United States. She won in 1916, to become the first woman in the House of Representatives.

Jeannette was totally against war. When President Wilson asked the Congress to vote to enter World War I, Jeannette voted no. She fought to get a bill passed in the House of Representatives that would offer a constitutional amendment giving women the right to vote. Although Jeannette suffered defeat in the next election, the amendment passed just after she left office.

After the war, Jeannette worked tirelessly for peace. She attended the Peace Conference in Zurich, Switzerland, where women from both sides of warring nations planned ways to prevent future wars. Jeannette also worked ten years as a lobbyist for the National Council for Prevention of War.

During the 1930s Adolf Hitler came into power in Germany. Jeannette realized that Europe and the United States were heading into war again. She moved back to Montana so she could run for Congress and try to keep the United States out of another war. Older people in Montana knew Jeannette, but the younger ones did not. She went to fifty-two of the fifty-six high schools in her district and spoke to students. The students then went home and talked to their parents about Jeannette Rankin's ideas. This kind of advertising worked for her, and she won easily.

The Japanese bombed Pearl Harbor on December 7, 1941. The next day, President Roosevelt called for a declaration of war. Jeannette's "nay" was the only one cast. Many people wrote abusive letters to her, but she never wavered in what she believed was the right thing to do. She lost the next election.

After World War II, Jeannette made many trips around the world, searching for an answer to the problem of war. Yet she gave no formal speeches until she was eighty-seven. In that year she spoke out against the war in Vietnam. Now many supported her. In January 1968, when she was eighty-eight years old, she led a peace march in Washington, D.C. She spoke at colleges and universities around the country, and the students backed her.

Jeannette was nearing ninety when she fell and broke her hip in Watkinsville, Georgia. She worked hard to regain the ability to walk because she had been invited to speak to Congress on her ninetieth birthday. She entered the chamber in a wheelchair but stood to give her talk, which was given without notes. Her one dream was to eliminate war, and she spent her entire life working for that purpose.

1. Make a list of five words or phrases that describe Jeannette Rankin. Compare your list with a partner's.
2. How are you like and unlike Jeannette Rankin?
3. What does Jeannette's life as a young person in Montana tell you about her and possibly other young women in that state one hundred years ago?
4. What is the most important phrase to you in the biography of Jeannette Rankin?

SOCIAL STUDIES

1. Jeannette moved to Georgia to be closer to Washington, D.C. Study a map to find out how much closer it was.
2. How many women are members of the House of Representatives this term? (See a recent almanac or other reference book for the data.)
3. Jeannette was devoted to eliminating war. If you were to run for Congress, to what main issue or cause would you devote your energy? Write a short campaign speech stating your stand on this issue.
4. Write a newspaper editorial with this topic: My view on whether our country should ever enter into war again.

FURTHER READING

Davidson, Sue. *A Heart in Politics: Jeannette Rankin and Patsy T. Mink.* Women Who Dared Series. Seattle, WA: Seal Press, 1994.

Stein, R. Conrad. *The Powers of Congress.* Cornerstones of Freedom Series. Chicago: Childrens Press, 1995.

Weber, Michael. *Our Congress.* I Know America Series. Brookfield, CT: The Millbrook Press, 1994.

ELEANOR ROOSEVELT ★ 1884–1962

Diplomat, Humanitarian, Writer

Two-year-old Eleanor kept close to her father and mother on the steamship. Suddenly, there was a wrenching shudder, and she became separated from them. The ship began to sink. Eleanor fell one way and then another during the turmoil. Finally, friendly hands lifted her above the ship's railing and dropped her into the loving arms of her father in a lifeboat below.

Eleanor's chin receded, which was probably why her aunt called her "the ugly duckling." Her spine was crooked, so she had to wear a bulky brace. The other members of Eleanor's family were handsome and beautiful, especially Anna, Eleanor's mother. Anna called her daughter "serious" and "old-fashioned." Eleanor thought herself "plain."

When Eleanor was fifteen, Grandmother Mary Hall sent her to Allenswood, a private school in England for young women. There Eleanor prepared for adulthood under headmistress Mademoiselle Souvestre, who believed that young women had to think for themselves. Eleanor learned from her that she needed to leave the world a much better place than the one she found.

Eleanor was ecstatic after she arrived at Allenswood, for everyone was friendly. Classes were conducted in French, which Eleanor had learned at six years of age at a convent school, and she excelled in her schoolwork.

Soon after her return to the United States, she met a distant cousin, Franklin Delano Roosevelt. They fell in love and Franklin proposed. About a year later, Eleanor married the handsome and witty Franklin.

At thirty-nine, Franklin contracted infantile paralysis (polio) and was confined to a wheelchair for the rest of his life. Eleanor became his legs, going places he could not go. Franklin later became president of the United States.

Eleanor Roosevelt was a different First Lady from the ones who had preceded her. She traveled around the country to find out how average citizens really felt about problems that faced them. She was the first wife of a president to drive her own car or to travel by airplane. She even crossed a dam in a cablecar and went with coal miners deep into a mine shaft to learn about their working conditions.

From 1935 to 1945 she wrote a five-hundred-word column for newspapers, six days a week, called "My Day." That's a total of over three thousand columns! She wrote them while she visited wounded servicemen in various parts of the world.

After her husband died, Eleanor continued to work for the United Nations on human rights. From 1945 to 1951, she served as a delegate to the United Nations General Assembly. She helped to write the Universal Declaration of Human Rights, which was adopted by the United Nations General Assembly in 1948.

Eleanor Roosevelt became known as the "guardian of the conscience of the world." She has been a role model for women leaders ever since.

1. What title would you give Eleanor Roosevelt's biography?

2. Why do you think Eleanor has been a role model for many women? List some qualities and achievements that make her a role model.

3. What to you is the most important paragraph in the biography of Eleanor Roosevelt? Why?

4. In a thesaurus or dictionary, find synonyms for the following words used in Eleanor's biography: turmoil, ecstatic, guardian, conscience.

SOCIAL STUDIES

1. From a reference book, read through the thirty articles in the Universal Declaration of Human Rights. Select the five you think are most important and read them aloud to a partner. Discuss what they mean.

2. Because of her work on human rights, Eleanor became known as "the guardian of the conscience of the world." Write five to ten sentences on what that phrase means.

3. With a partner, write your own short Declaration of Human Rights. How do you feel that each human being should be treated? What rights does each human being have?

4. Interview an older person who was living before or during World War II. Ask that person what he or she remembers about Eleanor Roosevelt and her husband, Franklin. Compare and contrast that information with the biography.

5. Write a letter from Eleanor Franklin, telling him about her feelings as she visits our wounded servicemen in the South Pacific during World War II.

FURTHER READING

Freedman, Russell. *Eleanor Roosevelt: A Life of Discovery*. New York: Clarion Books, 1993.

Jacobs, William Jay. *Eleanor Roosevelt: A Life of Happiness and Tears*. Tarrytown, NY: Marshall Cavendish, 1991.

Toor, Rachel. *Eleanor Roosevelt: Diplomat and Humanitarian*. American Women of Achievement. New York: Chelsea House Publishers, 1989.

Weidt, Maryann N. *Stateswoman to the World: A Story About Eleanor Roosevelt*. Minneapolis: Carolrhoda Books, 1991.

Explorer and Guide

As a small child, Sacagawea (meaning "Bird Woman") was promised in marriage by her Shoshone father to the son of another tribal member. She was to marry the man chosen for her when she was thirteen or fourteen years old. But when she was ten or eleven, the tribe traveled to Three Forks, now in the state of Montana, where three rivers came together and formed the Missouri River. There Minnetaree Indians attacked the tribe, captured Sacagawea, and sold her to a French-Canadian trader, Toussaint Charbonneau, who already had another Indian wife and a child.

Across the country, Thomas Jefferson, the president of the United States, asked Congress for twenty-five thousand dollars to outfit an exploration party to explore and look for a route to the Pacific Ocean by way of the Oregon Territory. Jefferson chose his private secretary, Captain Meriwether Lewis, to head the expedition. Lewis selected Lieutenant William Clark as his coleader.

Lewis and Clark took their men and supplies up the Missouri River by boat from St. Louis. They realized they would need horses to take their supplies over the Rocky Mountains. The Shoshone Indians lived in that area and had horses, but no one in the Lewis and Clark party could speak the Shoshone language. They hired Charbonneau as an interpreter for the Indians who spoke the Minnetaree language. The coleaders insisted that Charbonneau bring his wife Sacagawea, who spoke Shoshone. They needed Sacagawea as an interpreter to get hors-es for the crossing of the Continental Divide.

Early in 1805, not long before the expedition began, Sacagawea had had a baby. She called him Jean Baptiste and nicknamed him "Pomp." The two-month-old Pomp was bundled onto a cradle board and slung over Sacagawea's back for the long trip to the Pacific Ocean and back.

The men put a sail on their boats as they headed north and west up the Missouri River. A sudden wind blew one boat to its side and it filled with water. Books, medicines, and instruments spilled into the water and floated away. The frightened Charbonneau, who controlled the rudder, tried to jump overboard. One man threatened to shoot him if he did not take hold of the rudder and do his duty. With that encouragement, he complied. Meanwhile, Sacagawea leaned over the side of the boat and caught almost everything and brought it aboard.

In August the expedition met the Shoshones. Sacagawea entered the chief's tent after Lewis and Clark summoned her to come and interpret. As her eyes became accustomed to the dim light, she recognized that the chief was her brother! Horses were bought and the group headed over the Continental Divide. The explorers finally reached the Pacific after having tremendous difficulties.

Sacagawea was more than an interpreter. She was an essential member of this important expedition. When the expedition returned, Charbonneau received $500.33 as wages. Sacagawea, however, received no pay.

People of Purpose

1. Write Sacagawea's part in the Lewis and Clark expedition as a poem.
2. What two questions would you like to ask Sacagawea?
3. Draw a cartoon of the incident in which wind blew one of the expedition's boats over. Show Sacagawea, Charbonneau, and the man who threatened to shoot. Add speech or thought balloons.
4. If you could change the ending of the Lewis and Clark expedition, how would you do it?

SOCIAL STUDIES

1. In a reference book or textbook, find a map showing the route of the Lewis and Clark expedition. Did the group travel through a state where you now live or have visited? Which one(s)?
2. Trace your finger down the Continental Divide on a map. Which side of the Divide do you live on?
3. Point out places on the expedition's route where you imagine they faced great difficulty. Read more about the expedition to find out what hardships they actually encountered.

4. Read about the Shoshone Indians in a reference book. Share three interesting facts with the class.

FURTHER READING

Andrist, Ralph K. *To the Pacific with Lewis and Clark.* New York: American Heritage Publishing Co., 1967.

Gleiter, Jan, and Kathleen Thompson. *Sacagawea.* First Biographies Series. Austin, TX: Raintree Steck-Vaughn, 1995.

Jassem, Kate. *Sacajawea: Wilderness Guide.* Mahwah, NJ: Troll Communications, 1979.

O'Dell, Scott. *Streams to the River, River to the Sea.* New York: Houghton Mifflin, 1986.

Seymour, Flora Warren. *Sacagawea: American Pathfinder.* Childhoods of Famous Americans Series. New York: Aladdin Books, 1991.

JONAS SALK ★ 1914–1995

Research Scientist in Preventive Medicine

Jonas Salk was only twelve years old when he entered Townsend Harris Hall, a high school for gifted male students in New York City. The curriculum was rigorous. Students completed four years of course work in only three years.

At age fifteen Jonas was ready for college. His first goal was to become a lawyer. But, like many students, he changed his mind. He became interested in the medical field after taking a course in science. At age twenty-five he graduated from New York University School of Medicine with his M.D. degree. He promptly married Donna Lindsay, and in a few years they had three sons.

Jonas decided early in his schooling that he preferred to do medical research rather than become a family doctor or specialist. So in 1943 he went to the University of Michigan to work with one of his former teachers—Dr. Thomas Francis, Jr. Dr. Francis was developing a vaccine to control the influenza virus. During World War I, 850,000 Americans had died of influenza (flu). This number included 44,000 soldiers. By now the country was involved in World War II, and the U.S. government was concerned that another flu outbreak would harm and deplete its military forces. Jonas helped Dr. Francis develop a successful vaccine.

Later, Jonas turned his attention to *infantile poliomyelitis*, known as "polio," a paralyzing disease that seriously disabled both small children and adults. It was called *infantile* because of the effects it had on infants, but older people also contracted the disease. In 1952, 58,000 people developed polio in the United States alone. Even before that, President Franklin D. Roosevelt was crippled by polio when he was thirty-nine years old and spent the rest of his life in a wheelchair.

The citizens of this country were very concerned about polio. Every summer, outbreaks appeared around the country. On January 30, 1938, President Roosevelt's birthday, comedian Eddie Cantor suggested that all national radio programs donate thirty seconds of air time to ask people to send dimes to the White House in Washington, D.C. Eddie called it "The March of Dimes." The people responded. Bags of mail filled the corridors of the White House. The money totalled $1,823,045. Now there was enough money to help people with the disease, as well as money to do research to prevent polio.

Jonas and others worked diligently to develop vaccines so children and adults could be free of polio. Finally, the first safe vaccine was developed. Jonas inoculated himself, his wife, and his three boys (Peter, age nine; Darrell, age six; and Jonathan, age three) to show how safe he believed the new vaccine was. In 1955 the vaccine was licensed for use. Now children and adults do not get polio if they are inoculated with the vaccines that Jonas and others developed.

In 1963 Jonas opened the Salk Institute for Biological Studies in La Jolla, California. At the institute he continued to do research on viruses, write books and scientific articles, and advise the governments of many countries about public health matters.

1. Write a sixty-word paragraph about Jonas Salk. Exchange your paragraphs with a partner to read.

2. Do you suppose Jonas was a little fearful when he inoculated himself, his wife, and his children with the polio vaccine? Would you have been concerned if you were he?

3. What sort of person comes to your mind when you think of Jonas Salk? Write a description of his personality in three sentences.

4. Describe the people who would be most interested in this biography.

SOCIAL STUDIES

1. Talk to an older adult who remembers the outbreaks of flu and polio many years ago. Take notes and share what they said with the class.

2. Complete this sentence: If I were Jonas Salk, I would. . . .

3. What diseases would Jonas be trying to find vaccines for if he were alive today? Which disease should get the greatest amount of research funding? Why?

4. Can all men and women using the title "Doctor" help persons with medical problems? Why or why not?

FURTHER READING

Curson, Marjorie. *Jonas Salk. Great Lives Series*. Englewood Cliffs, NJ: Silver Burdett Press, 1990.

Curtis, Robert H. *Medicine: Great Lives*. Pioneers in Change Series. New York: Charles Scribner's Sons, 1993.

Sherrow, Victoria. *Jonas Salk*. Makers of Modern Science Series. New York: Facts on File, 1993.

lbert's friend suggested that shooting birds with a slingshot would be fun. Albert was hesitant but went along with the idea, and so the two young German boys headed out into the fields. They found a flock of birds in a tree, but as Albert drew back his sling with a stone in it, the church bells rang. All he could think of was the Bible verse his pastor father quoted: "Thou shall not kill." Immediately, he threw down the slingshot and shouted at the birds, frightening them away. He simply could not take a bird's life. Indeed, throughout his life, Albert Schweitzer could not stand seeing humans or animals suffer. He later called his philosophy "reverence for life."

At twenty-one Albert made a vow. He would study theology, philosophy, and music for nine years. After that, he would give his life for those who were suffering. He became a very knowledgeable man. Soon he was a clergyman and preached at St. Nicholas Church in Strasbourg. He also gave organ recitals. He met a young woman, Helene Bresslau. She too wanted to help others.

Still, Albert did not know what he was supposed to do to help humanity. He would soon be thirty. Then one day he read an article about the people in Africa who were ill and had no physician to treat them. He knew he must become a medical doctor. But the courses would take him seven years to complete. Helene changed her career as a social worker and took courses in nursing. She said she would wait for him, continue her studies, and then go with him to Africa.

When they finished their studies, Albert and Helene went to an area in West Africa now called Gabon. The mission station was called Lambaréné. It was on an island in the middle of the Ogowe River. They were told that a building would be erected for their hospital before they got there. But when they arrived, there was nothing but an old chicken coop to work in. Before he got off the boat, Albert saw people who were ill lining up to see him. He began cleaning the chicken coop so he would have a place to treat his patients. With the clinic up and running, many Africans were brought back to health.

World War I broke out. Albert was a German citizen working in a French province, and the French were at war with the Germans. The French made him and his wife prisoners of war and returned them to France. There, they were put in prison.

After the war, they again resumed their work in Africa. In 1919 they had a little girl and named her Rhena for the Rhine River in Germany. Helene could not stay in Africa because of ill health and the need to care for Rhena. Albert went back and forth to Switzerland to visit them. He played organ concerts in Europe to get more supplies for his hospital. When their daughter was older, Helene stayed with Albert at Lambaréné.

Helene died, and several years later, Albert, at ninety, passed away. He spent many years helping African people regain their health. For his humanitarian work, Albert received the Nobel Prize for peace in 1952.

People of Purpose

1. Make a list of ten words that describe Albert Schweitzer. Compare your list with a partner's.

2. What most inspired you about Albert's life? What would you like to imitate?

3. Do you think the Biblical command against killing covers birds and other animals? Why or why not? What does "reverence for life" mean to you? Write a paragraph, compose a poem, or draw a picture to describe the phrase.

4. Albert took a vow to help humanity when he was thirty. Do you believe there is a difference between a vow and a promise? If so, what is the difference?

SOCIAL STUDIES

1. Find Gabon (formerly French Equatorial Africa) on a map of Africa. What ocean forms its western border? Read an encyclopedia reference to Gabon. Share with the class why you would or would not want to visit Gabon.

2. What do you think Albert did with the $33,000 prize money from his Nobel Prize? What would you have done with it if you had won?

3. What do you think of the French decision to make Albert and Helene prisoners of war because they were Germans working in a French province in Africa? What could the French have done differently?

4. Albert was an accomplished musician, physician, philosopher, clergyman, missionary, and theological writer. Do you know of anyone who excels in each of these fields? Are you the kind of person who could excel in more than one field?

FURTHER READING

Cranford, Gail. *Albert Schweitzer*. What Made Them Great Series. Englewood Cliffs, NJ: Silver Burdett Press, 1990.

Curtis, Robert H. Medicine. *Great Lives Series*. New York: Charles Scribner's Sons, 1993.

Lantier, Patricia (adaptation of the book by James Bentley). *Albert Schweitzer*. People Who Made a Difference Series. Milwaukee, WI: Gareth Stevens Children's Books, 1990.

Robles, Harold E. *Albert Schweitzer: An Adventurer for Humanity*. Brookfield, CT: The Millbrook Press, 1994.

ELIZABETH CADY STANTON ★ 1815–1902

Leader in the Women's Rights Movement

Lizzie (short for Elizabeth) sat quietly in her father's law office listening to him as he counseled a woman about her right of ownership. She had purchased a farm with her own money. Her husband had died and in his will had deeded the farm to their son. The son did not take care of the farm and was mean to his mother. Nothing could be done, Judge Cady told her. When a woman married, her property became her husband's. A husband could do with it as he wished, even after his death.

After the woman left, Lizzie was angry. "How could this be?" she asked. "I'll cut the law out of all the law books." Judge Cady understood how Lizzie and many women of that day felt, but there was nothing anyone could do. The New York State Legislature had to change the law. And only men were elected to the legislature, and only they could vote.

When Lizzie was older, she met Henry Stanton. Henry traveled around the country speaking against slavery. He asked Lizzie to marry him, but Judge Cady would not give his consent. The judge thought Henry should get a real job. Even so, Henry and Lizzie eloped in 1840 and went to London, England, as delegates to the World Anti-Slavery Convention.

When they got to the meeting, the men voted not to allow the women to speak. They were asked to sit in the balcony behind a curtain. The women were furious and met afterward to discuss their problems. It was here that Lizzie met Lucretia Mott, a Quaker minister and abolitionist who was twenty-two years older than Lizzie. The women had much to talk about.

Back in the United States, Lucretia, Lizzie, and some others organized the Seneca Falls Women's Rights Convention. Lizzie wrote a Declaration of Sentiments, a statement on women's rights. The list of complaints the women composed covered a number of issues: women had no right to their own property if they married; only men had the power to divorce; women were denied equal education with men; and women could not vote.

In 1851 Lizzie and Susan B. Anthony met. They began a friendship that lasted for fifty years. Susan was a Quaker and was interested in temperance (not drinking alcoholic beverages) and the abolition of slavery. Now she also became interested in women's rights. Susan visited Lizzie and took care of her children while Lizzie wrote Susan's speeches.

On February 14, 1854, Lizzie finally had the opportunity to address the New York State legislature in the state capital at Albany. Before she gave her speech, she read it to her father. Judge Cady threatened to cut her out of his will if she gave it. But Lizzie was determined, and she told the men so. (Her father did not cut her out of his will.)

In 1888, on the fortieth anniversary of the Seneca Falls meeting, Lizzie gave the opening and closing speeches. With Susan, she continued to write speeches and work on a history of the women's movement. She did not live to see her ideas, such as the Nineteenth Amendment, made into law, but she felt sure that someday they would be.

1. From the list of four grievances mentioned in Elizabeth Cady Stanton's biography, which do you think is the most important? Why? Write a speech stating your opinion.
2. Read the first two paragraphs of the biography. Write a simple law that would allow women to keep their property when they marry. Compare your law with those of your classmates.
3. What would you have said to the men at the World Anti-Slavery Convention in London, England, if you went that distance and could not be involved in the meeting?

SOCIAL STUDIES

1. What did the Nineteenth Amendment to the Constitution provide? Why do you think it took so long for it to become law?
2. If Elizabeth could have come back in 1919 to address Congress on the day the Nineteenth Amendment passed, what would she have said?
3. Which of these three problems do you think was most serious in the 1800s: temperance (abstaining from alcoholic beverages); the abolition of slavery; or suffrage (women's and African Americans' right to vote)?
4. If only women were allowed to vote and hold elected office, how would life be different today?

FURTHER READING

Fritz, Jean. *You Want Women to Vote, Lizzie Stanton?* New York: G. P. Putnam's Sons, 1995.

MOTHER TERESA (Agnes Gonxha Bojaxhiu) 1910–1997

Reliever of Suffering

Agnes took her mother, Drana Bojaxhiu, aside from the dinner table and asked, "Mother, who are these people?" Even before her father died, when Agnes was eight, there were always friends or relatives, even strangers, eating with the family. Her mother's answer was always that they were relatives or our people. "Our people" were those in need. No one was turned away from the Bojaxhiu household.

Agnes Gonxha Bojaxhiu was born in Skopje, Macedonia, and learned from early childhood to live a life of giving and sharing. When she was eighteen, Agnes left home to become a Catholic nun. With her friend Betika, they made their way across Austria, Switzerland, and France, through London, and into Ireland. There, in the Loreto Order, she began to learn English. She took the name Sister Mary Teresa of the Child Jesus. Teresa, meaning the "little one," felt the call of God to go to India to teach and care for the poor and sick.

In 1946, when Teresa journeyed to Darjeeling in northern India, she felt God speak to her. His message was that she must leave the safety of the convent and live among the poor. A year later she received permission to put the plan into action. Teresa took four months of training in medicine from the Medical Missionary Sisters at Patna, along the Ganges River. She then returned to Calcutta to live in a hut. Her teaching began with five little children. Teresa taught them the alphabet by drawing letters in the dirt. This is how they learned to read and write. She also taught them to wash and comb their hair.

People began to notice her work. Someone gave her a chalkboard and chalk. Others brought chairs. Then girls she taught at the high school came to help. A new order of nuns started, and Teresa became "Mother Teresa." She called her new order the Congregation of the Missionaries of Charity.

The nuns in Mother Teresa's order wore white saris, as the poor did. But these saris had borders of blue and a small crucifix on the left shoulder. All the worldly goods these sisters owned were their saris, a rope girdle, a pair of sandals, underwear, a mattress, and a bucket to wash their clothes. They begged for food for the poor and for anything else they could get for them.

Pope Paul VI visited India in 1964. To move around the country, he was given a Lincoln Continental automobile by some Americans. In turn, the Pope gave it to Mother Teresa, and she gave it to a group of people to conduct a raffle. The raffle produced five times the car's worth. Mother Teresa used the money to start another hospital.

When she received the Nobel Prize for peace in 1971, Mother Teresa requested that the prize officials have no celebration dinner so that she could use that money for the poor. Even when flying to different places around the world, Teresa has asked that the leftover airline food be given to her for the hungry.

Mother Teresa, a reliever of suffering, was known as the "Saint of the Gutters." She died in 1997.

1. Write the letters of the word *mother* vertically. For each letter, write a word or phrase that describes Mother Teresa.
2. Without stopping, write about Mother Teresa for five minutes. Exchange your paper with a partner and compare what you wrote. What things were the same or different?
3. What does "Saint of the Gutters" mean to you? Could you be a saint of the gutters? Why or why not?
4. Do you know someone who comes close to being a Mother Teresa? What does that person do?

SOCIAL STUDIES

1. Study a map of India. Find Calcutta. Read about Calcutta in a reference book. Tell a classmate the most significant thing you discovered about the city.
2. Make a list of things that belong to you (stop at thirty!). How do they compare with the possessions that the sisters in Mother Teresa's order own? Why do you suppose they own so few possessions?
3. With Mother Teresa as your inspiration, brainstorm with a small group some simple things you can do to help those less fortunate than you. Make a list and read it every morning for a month.

FURTHER READING

Craig, Mary. *Mother Teresa*. Profiles Series. North Pomfret, VT: Trafalgar, 1991.

Schraff, Anne. *Women of Peace: Nobel Peace Prize Winners*. Hillside, NJ: Enslow Publishers, 1994.

Revolutionist General and Liberator

On the Caribbean island of Hispaniola, a small boy sat reading under the shade of a tree. The boy's original name was Pierre Dominique Toussaint-Bréda, but he later became known as Toussaint L'Ouverture. Toussaint was a slave. He remained one until he was nearly fifty years old.

A Frenchman visiting the plantation saw the boy reading and flew into a rage. Slaves were forbidden to read. He beat Toussaint so severely that his coat was bloodied. Toussaint did not resist, but he kept the coat as a reminder.

Toussaint's father, a former African chief, became the slave of a relatively humane French overseer on the Bréda plantation. The overseer allowed little Toussaint to learn formal French, read, write, and even take books from his library to read. From these books the boy learned of Julius Caesar's military campaigns and of famous generals such as Alexander the Great.

Toussaint's health was poor as a child. He gained strength by running over the mountains and learning to ride horses well. He gathered herbs and flowers and learned their uses in the healing process. The intelligent boy grew very strong and knowledgeable. In time, the other slaves and mulattoes recognized and respected him as a leader.

As he grew older, Toussaint became a trusted servant in the home of his French plantation master, near Cap Haïtien. He married and had two sons. Even so, he was considered a slave. Like other slaves, Toussaint desired freedom.

The French Revolution broke out in France in 1789. The slaves also revolted in Saint Domingue. Toussaint joined the revolt at first to help the injured and soon advanced to general. He taught the slaves army tactics he had learned from his reading, and they became a disciplined army. This army of former slaves defeated the French, captured the Spanish side of the island, and even defeated British troops who tried to invade the rich colony.

Toussaint frequently broke through his enemies' lines. This led a French governor of Saint Domingue (later Haiti) to say, "This man finds an opening everywhere." After that, Toussaint added "L'Ouverture" to his name, meaning "The Opening."

Napoleon came to power in France and sent 63,000 troops to Saint Domingue to reestablish slavery. By deceit, Napoleon's soldiers took Toussaint, his wife, and two sons to France. Then Napoleon separated the family. He allowed Toussaint to starve to death in a French prison in 1803.

Meanwhile, French soldiers could not keep Saint Domingue under control. The French lost because the slaves trained by Toussaint were transformed into an army. Diseases such as yellow fever and malaria also devastated the French army, whereas the black slaves and mulattoes were immune to these diseases. Finally, the black army surrounded the five thousand French soldiers, and they left the island. Toussaint L'Ouverture did not live to learn that the land he roamed as a child became the country called Haiti.

1. In a dictionary find the definitions of the following words used in the biography: *humane, overseer, indigo, plantation, mulatto.* Use them in sentences telling about Toussaint L'Ouverture. Compare your sentences with a partner's.
2. What skills did Toussaint have that made him of value in the revolt?
3. Napoleon's life ended in prison. What do you think Toussaint's reaction would have been if he could have known?
4. What would you like to change in the life of Toussaint? Rewrite the end of the biography.

SOCIAL STUDIES

1. Find the island of Hispaniola on a map. What large islands surround it? Where is Cap Haïtien located in Haiti? What body of water borders it?
2. Read about present-day Haiti in a reference book. Share three interesting facts with the class.
3. Toussaint's army defeated three major European armies. From which countries did they come? What does this tell you about Toussaint's leadership? Read about Alexander the Great in a reference book to learn what might have inspired Toussaint.

FURTHER READING

Hoobler, Thomas and Dorothy. *Toussaint L'Ouverture.* World Leaders Past & Present Series. New York: Chelsea House Publishers, 1990.

SOJOURNER TRUTH (Isabella Baumfree) ★ 1793–1883

Abolitionist and Orator

Isabella was an infant when her family's New York slave master, Colonel Hardenbergh, died. Now she and her brothers and sisters became someone else's property. Her father, James Baumfree, and her mother, Betsy, worried about their family, but they could do nothing about their situation because slaves were considered property and had no rights.

By the time she was nine, Isabella was growing tall and strong, just like her father. *Baumfree*, in the Low Dutch language spoken at that time in New York, meant "tree." She was tall and stately like a tree. Her mother, whom she called Mau-mau Bett, taught her to pray and be obedient.

New York passed a law that any slave born before July 4, 1799, would be freed in ten years. Dumont, her present owner, promised he would let her go in nine years if she worked hard. But he changed his mind shortly before the time for her freedom. He said that because she had been sick at times, she would have to work to make up that time. Isabella was furious and decided to leave anyway.

Before dawn one morning, she wrapped all her belongings in a white handkerchief, picked up her daughter, Sophia, and left. She found a family, the Van Wageners, who did not believe in slavery. They said they would take care of her. Dumont came to take her back, but the Van Wageners paid for the time she owed the Dumonts. Van Wagener gave Dumont twenty dollars for Isabella and five dollars for her child. They immediately set

Isabella free. Now, she could work as an employee for wages, not as a slave.

Isabella, now thirty years old and close to six feet tall, began speaking to groups of people about slavery and what she had experienced as a slave. She spent a lot of time traveling around the country giving speeches and decided to give herself a new name that would represent her better. For her first name she took "Sojourner," because she was on a journey. For her surname she chose "Truth," because truth was a name for the God whom she loved. Often she began her lectures, "Children, I speak to God and God speaks to me. . . ." Sojourner could neither read nor write, but she had memorized much of the Bible and would quote from it in her sermons, lectures, and speeches. She was known to say, "I cannot read a book but I can read people."

For years, she walked all over the Midwest, talking to groups about the horrors of slavery. There were many women who were involved in the issue of abolishing slavery at that time, but they had no voice in the process of changing laws. Many men did not think that women should be involved in organizing such things, even though the women were the ones doing most of the work. Sojourner soon realized that she needed to talk about women's rights too. And she did.

When the Civil War broke out, she helped in organizing and feeding black troops in the Union army. She spent her latter days with her children and grandchildren.

1. Isabella Baumfree took the name "Sojourner Truth." Write five to ten sentences on what her new name means and how it fits the life she led.
2. If Sojourner packed all her belongings in a white handkerchief, what do you suppose she had? What would you need in order to pack all your belongings?
3. What five words would you use to describe the Van Wageners?
4. What did Sojourner mean when she said, "I cannot read a book but I can read people"?

SOCIAL STUDIES

1. Who are some other women who helped the Union soldiers during the Civil War?
2. Write about what you now know life was like for slaves before slavery was abolished. If you wish, make up a story about a boy or girl who grew up as a slave.
3. Sojourner discovered that she needed to talk about women's rights as well as the abolition of slavery. Which issue do you think is more important? How are the two issues related to one another? Discuss these questions with a small group.

FURTHER READING

Altman, Susan. *Extraordinary Black Americans from Colonial to Contemporary Times*. Chicago: Childrens Press, 1989.

David A. Adler. *A Picture Book of Sojourner Truth*. New York: Holiday House, 1994.

Ortiz, Victoria. *Sojourner Truth, A Self-Made Woman*. New York: HarperCollins, 1986.

HARRIET TUBMAN ★ 1820?–1913

Leader of the Underground Railroad

In the South, during the time Harriet lived, a person who taught a slave to read or write could receive life in prison or even death. Slave owners knew that if slaves learned to read or write, they would soon want freedom, for reading opens a person's mind to all of life's possibilities. Harriet could not read but she learned about life in other ways.

Harriet learned from stories told her from the Bible. She learned from her father, Daddy Ben. He taught her about moss growing on the north side of oaks and pine trees, away from the sun's rays. Daddy Ben pointed to the North Star that waited in the night sky to guide slaves when no compass was available. He told her of freedom in the North, freedom from their slave master's oppression.

In her early teens, Harriet tried to stop an overseer from punishing a slave. The master threw a two-pound weight at her. It hit her in the forehead and fractured her skull. After that, she had blackouts and fell into a deep sleep at odd times.

By 1849 Harriet had escaped to Philadelphia and freedom. But she could not forget her mother and father, brothers, and friends who remained slaves in the South.

Nineteen times, Harriet stole into the South to rescue slaves. During the 1850s she helped over three hundred slaves find their way to freedom. She never lost a slave during those perilous times. Slave owners offered rewards totaling forty thousand dollars for her capture, dead or alive. Her feats were discussed in Northern abolitionist meetings and around fires in Southern slaves' quarters.

Harriet became the modern-day Moses to her people. The Biblical Moses led the Jews out of Egypt to freedom. Slaves heard her singing, "Oh go down, Moses, Way down in Egypt's land, Tell old Pharaoh, Let my people go." This was a signal that those who wanted to travel with her on the Underground Railroad would begin traveling Saturday night. By leaving on Saturday night, the slaves would not be missed by their owners until Monday morning. This gave them a head start before signs telling of their escape were printed and posted the following week.

After eight years of freedom, Harriet made a trip into the South to bring out her aging parents. Since they were not able to walk well, she quickly built a wagon of two wheels and a couple of boards to carry them. Then she tied the wagon to their old horse and off they went. She put them on a train with forged papers and sent them to safety. Harriet traveled through woods and fields and met them later.

During the Civil War, Harriet served as a scout, a spy, and a nurse. Before the war ended, Abraham Lincoln signed the Emancipation Proclamation officially freeing the slaves. At the end of three years of service, she received two hundred dollars from the government. She gave this to some ex-slaves so they could build a washhouse to support themselves.

Harriet died at ninety-two and was buried with full military honors. In 1978 the United States Postal Service issued a stamp in her honor.

1. List five things Harriet Tubman must have had in her personality to make her successful in what she did. Compare your list with a classmate's.

2. In a group, talk about Harriet Tubman. Write her a note telling her about your reaction to her life. Exchange papers and read the notes aloud.

3. With a classmate, create a dialogue between Harriet and her father, Daddy Ben, in which he tells her what he knows about the woods and sky.

4. How did the things Daddy Ben taught Harriet help her in sending slaves north on the Underground Railroad? Perform these as a play for your class.

SOCIAL STUDIES

1. Estimate how far it was and how long it would take slaves to travel to Philadelphia and Canada from various places in the South. What states would they travel through?

2. Read about the Underground Railroad in a reference book. Share with the class three things that interested you.

3. Imagine yourself as a slave traveling north at night and sleeping in holes, barns, haystacks, and swamps during the day. What would you think about? What would you feel? What would frighten you? Write about these experiences in a journal.

4. Look up the word *oppression* in a dictionary. With a partner, list some ways that slaves were oppressed. Then think of some forms of oppression that exist today. What would Harriet Tubman do about them?

FURTHER READING

Altman, Susan. *Extraordinary Black Americans from Colonial to Contemporary Times*. Chicago: Childrens Press, 1989.

Bial, Raymond. *The Underground Railroad*. Boston: Houghton Mifflin Company, 1995.

Blockson, Charles, L. *The Underground Railroad*. New York: Prentice-Hall Press, 1987.

Carlson, Judy. *Harriet Tubman: Call to Freedom*. Great Lives Series. New York: Fawcett Columbine, 1989.

Humphreville, Frances T. *Harriet Tubman: Flame of Freedom*. Boston: Houghton Mifflin Company, 1967.

Petry, Ann. *Harriet Tubman: Conductor on the Underground Railroad*. New York: HarperCollins Children's Books, 1996.

Stein, R. Conrad. *The Story of the Underground Railroad*. Cornerstones of Freedom Series. Chicago: Childrens Press, 1981.

Sterling, Dorothy. Freedom Train: *The Story of Harriet Tubman*. New York: Scholastic, 1987.

BOOKER T. WASHINGTON 1856–1915

Educator

Booker was born into slavery, but he grew up to be an advisor to three Presidents. Not until he was ten years old did he sleep in a real bed. His bed had been a grain sack on the floor. When Booker was a small child, his master had him carry his daughters' books to a school for white children only. Booker peeked in the classroom and saw the pupils studying. The scene stayed with him all his life. At that time it was against the law in the South to teach a slave to read, but he vowed he would learn.

Booker never knew his father. His stepfather, Washington Ferguson, left his slave owner and ran away to West Virginia. After the Civil War, when the slaves received their freedom, his stepfather wrote to Booker's mother to bring the family to West Virginia.

In West Virginia ten-year-old Booker and his brother worked in a salt mine with their stepfather. Booker begged to go to school. Finally, at the urging of his mother, the stepfather let Booker go to school part of the day, but he had to work in the salt mine too.

When Booker went to Hampton Institute in Virginia, he had no money. He worked as a janitor at the school to pay his way. A bill passed the Alabama State Legislature in 1881 to start a school for African American students in Tuskegee. Booker took charge of the new school.

When Booker arrived at Tuskegee, there was no building but there were thirty willing students, so he bought an old church shanty and began classes. He taught English, mathe-matics, and vocational subjects, such as growing cotton and building houses. His goal was to teach students how to make a living after they completed school. The school later became Tuskegee University.

One speech made Booker T. Washington instantly famous around the country. It became known as the "Atlanta Compromise." He told African Americans in the audience that they must stop demanding equal rights and simply get along with white people. Whites, he said, must give African Americans better jobs. Spreading out the fingers of his hand, he illustrated that African Americans and whites should be separate socially. Then he made a fist and said that on other matters of importance, such as "mutual progress," they must unite. Many whites and African Americans agreed with him; others did not.

Soon after, the Supreme Court ruled that "separate but equal" was the national guide for making government policy regarding the races. Some people at the time believed this was a good decision, although many others opposed it. The problem was that African Americans did not get equal treatment, particularly in education.

Booker T. Washington became the confidential advisor to President Theodore Roosevelt and even edited President William Howard Taft's inaugural address. Booker was the voice for African Americans for years. His school remains a fitting remembrance of his concern for African American youth.

1. Write on the top of a sheet of paper, "I will not forget. . . ." Then make a list of things you will not forget about Booker T. Washington.
2. From his biography, what scenes relating to schools and learning stick in your mind? Draw a picture or cartoon of one of those scenes.
3. What one thing did Booker do that you would not do?
4. Who do you know that would be interested in Booker's biography? Why would they be interested? Tell them about Booker in your own words.

SOCIAL STUDIES

1. Find Tuskegee on a map of Alabama. (It is east of Montgomery.) Read about Tuskegee University in an encyclopedia and tell your class a few things you learned about the institution.
2. Pretend you are Booker writing an advertisement for your new school. What would you write? How would you describe the school?
3. Choose three presidents of the United States that you would like to advise. Whom would you choose? What advice would you give them?
4. What do you think about Booker's "Atlanta Compromise"? How do you feel about the phrase "separate but equal"? Write a short speech agreeing or disagreeing with the phrase.

FURTHER READING

Altman, Susan. *Extraordinary Black Americans from Colonial to Contemporary Times*. Chicago: Childrens Press, 1989.

McKissack, Patricia and Fredrick. *Booker T. Washington: Leader and Educator*. Great African Americans Series. Hillside, NJ: Enslow Publishers, 1992.

McKissack, Patricia and Frederick. *The Story of Booker T. Washington*. Cornerstones of Freedom Series. Chicago: Childrens Press, 1991.

Patterson, Lillie. *Booker T. Washington: Leader of His People*. Discovery Biographies Series. New York: Chelsea Juniors, 1991.

Roberts, Jack L. *Booker T. Washington: Educator and Leader*. Gateway Civil Rights Series. Brookfield, CT: The Millbrook Press, 1995.

Schroeder, Alan. *Booker T. Washington*. Black Americans of Achievement Series. New York: Chelsea House Publishers, 1992.

YUNG WING ★ 1828–1912

Diplomat, Educator, Writer

Yung Wing was in his first year of school in Macao. His teacher was an English woman, a missionary to China. The year was 1834. His teacher took a special interest in Yung, for he was very small, the youngest in school, and away from his parents. She put him with a class of girls.

Yung was adventurous and planned an escape with six of the girls. He wanted to return home. After breakfast one day, the group stole away in a boat. They were halfway across the channel when they were discovered.

Yung lost none of his organizational skills or his brilliance over the years. When he was older, he was chosen to attend a school in the United States that would prepare him for college. He did well and asked his parents if he might stay on and go to Yale College (later Yale University). They reluctantly agreed. In 1850 Yung became the first Chinese to enroll at Yale, and actually the first Chinese ever to enroll in any U.S. college. He enjoyed his years there so much that in 1883 he became a naturalized citizen of the United States.

Yung returned home and told his mother: *"I am the first Chinese to graduate from Yale College, and that being the case, you have the honor of being the first and only mother out of the countless millions of mothers in China at this time, who can claim the honor of having a son who is the first Chinese graduate of a first-class American college. Such an honor is a rare thing to possess."*

When he returned to the United States, he met Mary Kellogg, married her, and had two sons with her. Yung spoke fluent English and was an excellent negotiator. The Chinese leaders made Yung an associate minister to its first permanent trade mission in the United States.

But Yung was offended at the way the United States was mistreating Chinese workers, particularly in the building of America's first transatlantic railway. He spoke out against the treatment of his people. Meanwhile, the Chinese government thought that Wing was making Chinese students more interested in the American way of life than the Chinese way. They called him home to China. His wife, after a serious illness, passed away in the United States. Yung returned to the United States, raised his two boys, wrote, and lectured.

For fifty years Yung was a United States citizen. Then he received a telegram from the State Department saying that his citizenship in the United States had been revoked. The authorities said that a change in the naturalization law made his application incorrect. He had to leave the country.

Yung left but soon slipped back into the United States and lived near his sons, who now had families in Connecticut. A few years later in 1909, he wrote his autobiography, *My Life in China and America*, the first Asian American to write an autobiography in English. As a diplomat, educator, and writer, Yung Wing brought honor to both of his countries.

1. From your reading of Yung Wing's biography, what instances in his life indicate that he had negotiating skills that the government of China could use? With a small group, make a list of rules for a negotiator to follow.

2. Read aloud the words Yung Wing used to tell his mother about graduating from Yale College. Play the part of Yung Wing and have a classmate play the part of Yung's mother. What would each say? Judging by the way Yung talked to his mother, how would they say it?

3. How did you feel when you read that Yung Wing had to return to China because of a change in the naturalization law? How did you feel about his slipping back into the country illegally so he could be with his sons and grandchildren?

SOCIAL STUDIES

1. Find Macao on a map of China. Read about it in a reference book and share three interesting facts with the class.

2. When was Yale University founded and where is it located? Read about the school in a reference book.

3. Of all the universities in the United States and elsewhere, which one would you prefer to attend? Why? Where is it located and when was it founded?

4. In a reference book, find out how a person can become a U.S. citizen. With your class, invite a naturalized U.S. citizen to come and speak about his or her experience. Prepare some questions to ask him or her.

FURTHER READING

Ferroa, Peggy. *China*. Cultures of the World Series. New York: Marshall Cavendish, 1991.

Kent, Deborah. *China: Old Ways Meet New*. Exploring Cultures of the World Series. New York: Benchmark Books, 1996.

Sinnott, Susan. *Extraordinary Asian Pacific Americans*. Chicago: Childrens Press, 1993.

EMILIANO ZAPATA

Revolutionary and Agrarian Reformer

Before he was twelve, Emiliano learned to jump his horse over stone walls in the village of Anenecuilco, Mexico. If he fell, his parents did not give him sympathy. His uncle took him deer hunting in the mountainous areas of the state of Morelos, just south of the capital, Mexico City, and taught him to shoot.

In each Mexican village, villagers would vote for a president of their village council. Generally, presidents were older men who grew up in the small towns, but the villagers in the town where Emiliano lived recognized his leadership qualities. At the age of thirty, he became the village president.

Mexico had a population of twelve million people, of which ten million were Indians or *mestizos*—those with a mixture of Indian and Spanish blood. The few landowners owned most of the land, lived in beautiful haciendas, and sent their children abroad to study. They took more and more land from the mestizos to grow sugarcane for exporting. Ninety-six percent of Mexico's rural families had no land and received low wages.

Francisco Madero became president of Mexico but did not keep his promise to begin land reform. Emiliano, then a wiry 120 pounds, became angry. With the help of a school teacher, Otilio Montaño, he wrote the *Plan of Ayala*. The plan called for the overthrow of Madero and the return of the land to the rightful owners, the common citizens. The plan was published by a Mexico City newspaper and received wide circulation. Revolts developed all over southern Mexico. When the fighting

died down, the men went back to their farms to plant crops for the coming harvest.

The state of Morelos prospered greatly under Emiliano's leadership. The people had enough beans and corn to eat, with some left over to sell. The villagers not only raised meat, fruits, and vegetables, they grew sugarcane as well. The profits paid the soldiers' hospital bills and gave the widows of soldiers killed in battle a pension.

Large companies in the United States and other foreign investors were unhappy with Mexico's government. The United States government preferred a dictator to a moderate such as Madero. The Mexican government was overthrown and Madero was shot.

The new president, General Victoriano Huerta, had the backing of the Mexican army. Woodrow Wilson, then president of the United States, refused to recognize the government of Huerta. Another Mexican president, Venustiano Carranza, came to power, and a new constitution was adopted. Carranza feared Emiliano's great popularity with his people.

In 1919 Emiliano was told that some government troops wanted to defect to his side. Although he was skeptical, he went to accept them as part of his army. He was betrayed when troops shot two rifle volleys into his back. He became an instant martyr.

Emiliano Zapata loved the Mexican people and gave his life for them. He showed them by his actions how they could make a better life for themselves.

People of Purpose

1. Fold a paper lengthwise. Select any five sentences or phrases from Emiliano Zapata's biography and write them in the left column. In the right column, opposite each sentence or phrase, write your reaction. Exchange papers with a classmate and discuss what you wrote.

2. Think of three titles you could give to a book-length biography of Emiliano Zapata.

3. If Emiliano came to your class or home, what two questions would you ask him? What two questions would he ask you?

4. Read a biography of Crazy Horse. In what ways is Emiliano Zapata similar to Crazy Horse? How are they different?

SOCIAL STUDIES

1. Find the state of Morelos, south of Mexico City, on a map. Read about the city and the state and report three things that you find interesting.

2. With a partner, read about the Mexican Revolution in a reference book. How long did it last? Who was fighting whom? Share three interesting facts about it with the class.

3. How does your dictionary define *martyr*? Does Emiliano Zapata fit the description of a martyr? In what way?

FURTHER READING

Ragan, John David. *Emiliano Zapata*. World Leaders Past & Present Series. New York: Chelsea House Publishers, 1989.

JANE ADDAMS
Social Studies
1. Lake Michigan
2. Marie Curie; Poland, then France

KONRAD ADENAUER
Social Studies
1. Western Germany
2. Countries: Poland, Czech Republic, Austria, Switzerland, France, Luxembourg, Belgium, Netherlands, Denmark; North Sea, Baltic Sea
3. 1989

CORAZON AQUINO
Social Studies
1. Luzon
2. West: South China Sea; East: Philippine Sea

KEMAL ATATÜRK
Social Studies
1. Mediterranean Sea, Aegean Sea, Black Sea
3. Islam; Mohammed

JOHN JAMES AUDUBON
Reading
4. Ambidextrous

CLARA BARTON
Social Studies
2. A red cross on a white background for most countries; a red crescent on a white background for Muslim countries; a red Star of David on a white background for Israel

ELIZABETH BLACKWELL
Social Studies
1. Appalachian

KIT CARSON
Social Studies
1. Southwest
3. In the South, and east of the Mississippi River

RACHEL CARSON
Reading
2. To be extremely careful and precise

CÉSAR CHÁVEZ
Social Studies
4. Pesticide residue can make a person ill. Wash fresh vegetables thoroughly.

CHIANG KAI-SHEK
Social Studies
1c. Vietnam, Laos, Myanmar (Burma), India, Bhutan, Nepal, Pakistan, Afghanistan, Tajikistan, Kirghizia (Kyrgyzstan), Kazakhstan, Russia (Russian Federation), Mongolia, North Korea
1d. Ninety miles

JACQUES COUSTEAU
Social Studies
1. Pacific Ocean, Atlantic Ocean, Indian Ocean; Arctic Ocean
3. Indian Ocean

CRAZY HORSE
Social Studies
2. United States Army soldiers whose uniforms were blue

BILLIE DAVIS
Social Studies
1. Twenty-two

DOROTHEA LYNDE DIX
Reading
4. A person who donates money and time to worthy charities

AMELIA EARHART
Reading
2. For comfort and ease of movement
Social Studies
1. To circle the earth staying as close to the equator as possible

THOMAS A. EDISON
Social Studies
1. To receive a government grant that gives one the sole right to manufacture and sell a new invention for a set number of years

ALBERT EINSTEIN
Social Studies
2. 1921; the study of matter, energy, and their interaction

ANNE FRANK
Social Studies
1. Sea: North Sea; countries: Belgium, Germany

GEORGE WASHINGTON GOETHALS
Social Studies
1. Builds military bridges, roads, airfields, military camps, and other installations; clears mines and booby traps; and demolishs roads and bridges

MATTHEW HENSON
Social Studies
4. Twenty-four hours; the sun never sets from March 20 to September 23

DANIEL K. INOUYE
Social Studies
1. Juris Doctor
2. Two years
3. Six years
4. Approximately 2,400 miles (3,860 kilometers)

MAHALIA JACKSON
Social Studies
1. Illinois, Kentucky, Tennessee, Mississippi, Louisiana

ANN LANDERS
Reading
2. Fraternal twins: may be two brothers, two sisters, or a brother and a sister, with each sibling having a different genetic makeup; identical twins: are of the same sex and have identical genetic makeup
Social Studies
4. An agency that sells articles and cartoons for publication in a number of newspapers or magazines

LYDIA LILIUOKALANI
Reading
4. Hawaiian alphabet: twelve letters; English alphabet: twenty-six letters
aloha: love, greetings, welcome, farewell
Social Studies
1. 132 islands

JULIETTE GORDON LOW
Reading
3. A private school for instructing young girls on how to act properly in social situations
Social Studies
1. Atlantic Ocean

DOLLEY PAYNE MADISON
Social Studies
1. 1901; President Theodore Roosevelt

NELSON ROLIHLAHLA MANDELA
Social Studies
1. Namibia, Botswana, Zimbabwe, Mozambique, Swaziland

PATSY TAKEMOTO MINK
Social Studies
1. Every two years
2. 435 members

MARIA MITCHELL
Social Studies
3. Latitude: horizontally east and west; longitude: vertically north and south
4. About 2061

JULIA MORGAN
Social Studies
4. North

JOHN MUIR
Reading
2. Streets lined with tall buildings
Social Studies
1. North Sea; large areas of open, rolling land.
2. Travel westward over the frontier was considered more difficult than sailing the long way around. The Panama Canal was not in operation officially until July 12, 1920.
4. Erosion takes away the topsoil.

MARGARET MURIE
Social Studies
4. Destruction of their habitat

FLORENCE NIGHTINGALE
Social Studies
1. South
2. Black Sea

ALFRED NOBEL
Social Studies
2. Six awards; physics, chemistry, medicine, literature, economics, and peace

SANDRA DAY O'CONNOR
Reading
3. Abigail wrote to her husband to "remember the ladies" as he helped draft the United States Constitution. The amended Constitution allowed Sandra to become a justice.
Social Studies
2. Determines whether federal, state, and local governments act according to the Constitution of the United States. Nine justices—a chief justice and eight associate justices—appointed by the president with the advice and consent of the Senate.

JOSEPH PULITZER
Social Studies
1. Slovakia, Ukraine, Romania, Yugoslavia, Croatia, Slovenia, Austria
3. The editorial, or "opinion" pages

JONAS SALK
Social Studies
4. No. Some doctors have their degrees in chemistry, education, theology, and so on.

ALBERT SCHWEITZER
Social Studies
1. Atlantic Ocean
2. Expanded his hospital and established a leper colony

ELIZABETH CADY STANTON
Social Studies
1. Women's right to vote

FRANÇOIS-DOMINIQUE TOUSSAINT L'OUVERTURE
Reading
2. He knew of army tactics and the healing properties of herbs.
Social Studies
1. Cuba, Jamaica, Puerto Rico; north coast of Haiti; Atlantic Ocean
3. France, Spain, Great Britain

SOJOURNER TRUTH
Social Studies
1. Clara Barton, Elizabeth Blackwell, Dorothea Lynde Dix

YUNG WING
Social Studies
2. 1701; New Haven, Connecticut

INDEX BY CAREERS & OCCUPATIONS